CELEBRATING 20 YEARS
OF GREAT RESULTS

George Gallup Jr.

ama

AREA MARKETING/RESEARCH ASSOCIATES

October 16, 1987

D0929128

THE
GREAT
AMERICAN
SUCCESS
STORY

THE GREAT AMERICAN SUCCESS STORY

Factors That Affect Achievement

George Gallup, Jr.
Alec M. Gallup

with William Proctor

DOW JONES-IRWIN
Homewood, Illinois 60430

ISBN 0–87094–601–3
Library of Congress Catalog Card No. 85–72469
Printed in the United States of America

1 2 3 4 5 6 7 8 9 0   K   3 2 1 0 9 8 7 6

PREFACE

The idea of doing a book on success came to me a few years ago as I worked on a biography of my father, the late George Gallup, who founded the Gallup Poll.

Dr. Gallup was clearly a success. In the 1930s he gained recognition as one of the world's leading public opinion researchers. Consequently, he was included in all the leading biographical listings, including Marquis' *Who's Who In America*, which is used as a major source for this book. As I tried to determine the factors in my father's background that led to his accomplishments, it struck me that he was an example of a far wider phenomenon—one that could be explored and explained through a carefully designed sample of successful people.

There were a number of factors about my father's childhood that seemed to destine him for achievement. His hometown of Jefferson, Iowa, where he was born in 1901, has an ethos that promoted success among its young people. People in Jefferson placed a top priority on a good education. Virtually all local high school students went on to college, a fact that set the town apart from other American towns in the early 20th century. Residents also placed a high premium on hard work. My father had to contribute to the family income from a young age. When he was 10, he started a milk route with his brother John. They went out every morning in a horse-drawn cart to make deliveries to their customers.

Another important factor is that he was an insatiable

reader from childhood on. Although his mother was strict in many ways, she allowed him to stay up late at night as long as he was reading a book. And more often than not, that's what he did every night.

I remember my father as a true intellectual in the classic sense of the word. He was interested in ideas more than events or people-related issues and he discovered at an early age the pleasures of using his mind.

I learned a great deal from my father and I began to think, "Wouldn't it be valuable to be able to learn from *many* people like him—people who had achieved great things in a variety of fields?"

The Gallup Poll was the ideal instrument to probe the minds of a large number of successful people. And Marquis' *Who's Who In America* represented the best source for selecting a sample of those individuals.

This book provides an opportunity for individual readers to sit down for a few hours with the most successful people in America—presidents of the largest corporations, top artists and writers, military leaders, prize-winning scientists, great educators, and important members of the clergy. The few hours you spend perusing the following pages represent a distillation of over 1,000 hours of in-depth conversation with the most important and successful people in the United States, concerning their thoughts about the meaning of success and how they attained it.

One of the lessons of this book is that anyone can be a success! Although many people automatically assign themselves to the status of an *also-ran,* the results of our study show that most of us have the potential to be high achievers. There's no reason to rationalize the success of others by offering such excuses as, "She has a silver spoon in her mouth" or "He always gets all the breaks." Success is within your grasp if you'll just take steps to achieve it!

For example, common sense, which high achievers consider the most important personal characteristic for success, is something upon which we all draw. Also, successful people place a lot of importance on old-fashioned virtues like hard work, the desire to excel, goal setting, and caring about others.

Of course, success isn't something a person can always control. Many times, we found, success arose from some combination of acquired traits *plus* a kind of "X" factor—such as luck, accident of birth, a teacher's early influence, an exceptionally high intelligence, or religious faith. I remember a newspaper editor who said he owed his success to "hard work, perseverance, and the fact that my father owns the company."

Yet, our study seems to say that, while there are no shortcuts, success is possible for most people as long as they're willing to plan and work toward it.

Another point to keep in mind is what might be called the *maverick factor*. This refers to the many exceptions, represented as small percentages of the total, that emerge from any broad study or survey. *Most* of the successful people we questioned said they weren't motivated by money. But a *few* were. Most had high IQs, but some were only average. Most had at least a college education—but not all did.

In any case, we hope every reader will find this book instructive and perhaps even inspiring. Above all, if you do reach a high level of achievement, we trust you'll be motivated to use your position for the good of others, as most of these successful people have.

One of the happiest surprises for me was that the achievers we interviewed are not overly aggressive or insensitive people who are only out for "number one." In our society, we tend to admire the wheeler-dealer who scores by aggressive but not necessarily admirable behavior. In contrast, our respondents prove that personal success often involves a great social consciousness as well. They care about others, they volunteer their time to aid the needy, and the large majority give money to charity.

I find such results reassuring. In a way, the most successful people in our society seem to *deserve* success. On many levels, they are worthy of emulation.

So what we have here is an affirmation of the old-fashioned American credo that hard work and determination pay off. But at the same time, *The Great American Success Story* doesn't tell us to succeed at all costs. The greatest achievers are concerned citizens who have contributed a great deal, not only in their own fields, but in a variety of voluntary activities—and this, I believe is one of the keys to America's strength.

George Gallup, Jr.
Princeton, New Jersey

ACKNOWLEDGMENTS

Our thanks are owed Sarah Van Allen, Marie Swirsky, Coleen McMurray, and Mike Helmstadter. Hase Shannon Research Associates, Inc. and Howard Berger Associates were enormously helpful in processing the survey data and making special tabulations. And a profound debt of gratitude is owed to Michael Jacobs of Howard Berger Associates who tabulated the data, and Stuart Duncan, vice president of Hase Shannon, who played a major role in the development and administration of the survey.

We would also like to thank Marquis Who's Who, Inc., publishers of *Who's Who in America* for use of information in the 43rd edition of *Who's Who in America*.

TABLE OF CONTENTS

Part I

THE
KEYS TO
SUCCESS

CHAPTER

WHAT IS SUCCESS?

The hope of the future rests with the citizen. To be effective, he must be well informed, and he must discover ways of making better use of his own great mental capacities and those of his fellow men. . . . Man has scarcely begun to make use of his almost limitless brain power, either individually or collectively.

George Gallup, Sr. (from *The Miracle Ahead,* New York: Harper & Row, 1964, pp. 202–3).

You're sure you want it. You probably think you haven't got it. Even if you do have it, you want more of it. What is it? Money? Fame? Power? Great achievement?

In part, perhaps. But what you're *really* looking for runs into deeper waters. It may be all those material and worldly things, or it may be none of them, depending on your viewpoint.

In short, if you're like most people, what you really want in life is *success*. But like all other great goals and virtues of life—including love, joy, or happiness—the problem first is defining exactly what success is. Then, after you understand the nature of this Holy Grail you're in quest of, the question becomes, "How do I get it?"

The quicksilver quality of success and of savoring its benefits has long been pondered by our most sensitive thinkers. Emily Dickinson, for instance, wrote:

> "Success is counted sweetest
> By those who ne'er succeed."

There's little doubt that ambitious folks who lack success tend to crave it most, and this hunger may emerge in a variety of forms. The one who aspires strongly to success may dwell on the subject in conversations; he may devour every how-to article and achievement-oriented book he can lay his hands on. Or she may formulate detailed strategies about the best way to "get to the top" or "grab the brass ring" or "go for the gold."

Yet, more often than not, success, like joy and happiness, tends to slip up on us through people and paths that have not been part of our master plan. Even after a successful person makes it, he may not be able to tell you exactly how it happened—though plenty of those who observed the progress are sure *they* know. A consummate 19th-century quipster, John Churton Collins, made the point rather ironically when he said, "The secret of success in life is known only to those who have not succeeded."

So trying to answer a question like "What is success?" is risky business. But this element of difficulty and uncertainty in nailing down a definition is one of the things that has fascinated us as we've probed into the meaning of success.

For example, if you asked John Marks Templeton, who has been called the world's greatest living investor, what success means for him, he would certainly point to the fact that his Templeton Growth Fund was the most successful public mutual fund in the world for the two decades spanning the 1960s and 1970s.

But Templeton's view of success goes far beyond outward achievements and the accumulation of money. He stresses what he calls "stewardship," the idea that all his assets and

4

talents have been given to him by others (i.e., those investing in his mutual funds) and by God. As a result, he feels he has been entrusted with the weighty responsibility of managing those assets and talents so that their use is maximized for the common good. Success, then, can be measured by the degree to which he helps and enriches others, even as he is helping himself.

The renowned entertainer and TV personality Art Linkletter conceives of success in somewhat the same way. He sees an outward aspect to his success in that, during his early years, he actually traveled around the country as a hobo. But now, as he puts it, "I'm a multimillionaire, with money coming in from show business, manufacturing, oil and gas, mining, and real estate projects in the United States and Australia."

Still, success doesn't end there for Linkletter. There's also an inner dimension involving spiritual growth, personal peace, and emotional equilibrium. And he's a family man who puts great stock in his relationships. Success for Linkletter is indeed a comprehensive package.

We've discovered an incredibly varied view of success as we've conducted interviews with accomplished Americans during the past couple of years. The results have turned out to be highly instructive in revealing exactly what success is— and how the average person might go about getting it.

For example, in answering a number of questions we put to him, one prominent writer and editor illustrated some of the problems we all have as we try to get a firm handle on the meaning of success. When we asked what he considered to be evidence of his personal success, he replied in rather traditional, objective terms: "Publication in prestigious journals. Book publication. Editorship of a national magazine."

He also had a rather predictable response when we asked what he regarded as the formula for success in his field: "Ability (talent). Continuous hard work. Stubborn determination. Pure luck."

With an income in the six-figure range and a very satisfying family and personal life, this writer-editor's outlook on life was exactly what we would have expected it to be: "Very happy," he told us.

Yet obviously, success wasn't something that had come easily to him. In advising young people who might want to enter his field, he said, "Since this is the field of creative writing, you must be sure it is what you *can* do and *must* do. It is high risk. Be willing to face intensive work and rejection after rejection."

He also put a high premium on setting the right priorities: "Forget the drive for the dollar. Go where your heart and mind take you. Then work at it."

When we asked him to expand further on his ideas about his fundamental definition of success, an ambivalent and even troubled tone began to surface. "Success is a destructive concept," this writer-editor declared. "It has come to be inextricably entangled with celebrity, notoriety, fame, and, of course, riches.

"Is a lawyer who puts his ability and training at the service of the indigent less successful than one who wins fame and riches in the divorce courts or in criminal cases? Was Pearl Buck, who won the Nobel prize, more 'successful' than James Joyce, who did not?

"In certain areas—the sciences, for example—success can be measured by specific kinds of progress. In business, money is the critical measure. But what is the measure in the humanities? In the arts? Perhaps personal integrity is the measure that really counts—the sense of true effort, of willingness to risk, of honest accomplishment. These supply the satisfaction that one's life is being well used. What else is needed?"

Clearly, when you ask "What is success?" you run into a number of problems, as this quite successful man suggests. For one thing, some people may assume that there must be one general definition or standard of success that all reasonable men and women should accept. Actually, we've found there *isn't* just one definition of success that's generally accepted across the board among high achievers.

Also, as we've seen, some people define success objectively, as a certain level of achievement, prominence, or recognition. Others, like the above writer-editor, stress that true success is really a *subjective* phenomenon—a status that is wrapped up with an inner sense of satisfaction, happiness, and fulfillment.

Many others, like John Templeton and Art Linkletter, see success as a combination of both the objective and the subjective; that is, you're not truly successful unless you've (1) reached a certain high level of professional or outward accomplishment and (2) begun to *feel* satisfied and successful to boot.

During the past few decades at the Gallup Organization, we've conducted many surveys and investigations into topics that bear on the meaning of success. But for this book, we've gone even further. For the first time, we've focused in depth on the topic, probing attitudes and personal traits of prominent people and giving them wide latitude to tell their personal stories.

Specifically, we've used Marquis' *Who's Who In America*, now in its 83d year of publication, as our basic source. To ensure the greatest degree of accuracy, a survey sample approach has been employed—that is, the names of those we've polled have been picked by a scientific, random method so as to preclude any sort of bias. Also, we've selected a large survey sample of 1,500 people to interview. This ensures that our results are correct within a narrow margin of error.

But why *Who's Who?*

This brings us back to our basic question about what exactly is success. Obviously, many people who haven't been chosen by Marquis' *Who's Who* are successful by a variety of valid yardsticks.

Still, we know for a fact that the people who compile this publication make every effort to fulfill the objective they've stated at the beginning of their two-volume set of prominent names: "To chronicle the lives of individuals whose achievements to society make them subjects of interest and inquiry."

Specifically, an individual desire to be listed isn't sufficient reason for inclusion. Neither is wealth nor social position. The main criterion is current achievement in a given field. Once a biographee has retired from active participation in a career or other activity, he or she is dropped from the listing.

To put it another way, there are two main considerations for determining who will be admitted to the listing: (1) the position of responsibility that the person has held or (2) the level of significant achievement attained in the career or noteworthy activity.

The first standard is objective; that is, you'll be included in the list if you reach a certain level in the federal government, in a major religious denomination, in a large corporation, or in some similar organization. The second standard is somewhat more subjective; but even here, objective criteria are important. So, *Who's Who* includes artists whose works hang in major museums and professors who have made major contributions to their fields.

The responses we received about the basic meaning of success were as varied, profound, and feisty as the people and professions included in the listings. Now, let us introduce you to four representative characters who have played a part in helping us formulate the Great American Success Story. They have some especially fascinating thoughts to offer on what true success involves.

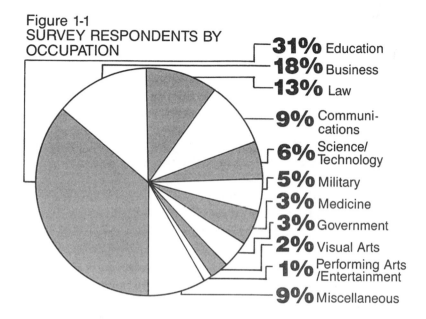

Figure 1-1
SURVEY RESPONDENTS BY
OCCUPATION

31% Education
18% Business
13% Law
9% Communi-
cations
6% Science/
Technology
5% Military
3% Medicine
3% Government
2% Visual Arts
1% Performing Arts
/Entertainment
9% Miscellaneous

THE FILM CRITIC

This internationally known film reviewer, who makes between $100,000 and $200,000 a year, told us, "I detest ques-
tionnaires and obviously cannot resist them. How objective
can one get? I want to know if other 'successful' people are as
full of themselves as I appear in my responses. But nowhere
did you ask about modesty—or humility. I'd rate myself well
on those."

This woman counts among the main evidences of her success the fact that she's known internationally in her field and
has been constantly employed by top news and TV media
for 22 years. "A critic is nothing without a voice," she says.

But even in the midst of this exuberant savoring of her

success, there's a plaintive note. "Know what you're getting into," she advises young people who are considering film criticism. "It's not so exciting or interesting or glamorous as the layman believes."

THE MOVING COMPANY PRESIDENT

This 60-year-old man, who is also a lawyer, was more uncomfortable than the film critic with what he perceived as current definitions of success.

He told us, "Any prominence or recognition I might have received came quite by accident and not by design or as a goal. Indeed, the standards or values by which success is now defined or recognized are generally alien to those I learned as a boy—and [those standards] have been abandoned in an increasingly materialistic and artificial society. Now, success seems to be based on mindless, and frequently ruthless, achievement of personal goals, followed by conspicuous consumption."

At one point, he also complained about our questionnaire: "I have a basic quarrel with your premise that success is measured by one's gaining prominence and recognition in his or her field of endeavor. Many *truly* successful people in this world never sought nor achieved—indeed, have refused and avoided such achievement. A knowledge of basic self-worth requires no recognition by others."

Yet, there was some inconsistency in his thinking on this point. In answer to a question about what he regarded as evidence of his personal success, he replied: "Respect and affection of peers, family, and those who engage in making such judgments (e.g., Marquis' *Who's Who* in America, In the World, In American Law)."

Indeed, it's hard, if not impossible, to escape some outward standard by which success may be judged. Otherwise, there's a tendency to equate success with inner peace, tranquility, and feelings of fulfillment even though there may be absolutely no perceptible forward movement in a person's career or contributions to society. In other words, success may become just another facet of complacency.

But still, this lawyer-executive has earned three university degrees, is clearly a thoughtful person. He said the books that had the most impact on his life were Thoreau's *On Walden Pond* and the Bible. And the way he prefers to spend his free time is in places and activities that promote rumination: fishing, hunting, and scenic driving.

Perhaps it's this meditative inclination that has given rise to this man's reservations and uncertainties about the significance of his level of achievement. Certainly, he indicated he regards himself as successful: When asked to rate his level of success on a scale of zero to 10, with 10 being the highest degree of success, he put himself in the 10 category. In contrast, 87 percent of the high achievers we polled rated themselves at lower levels of success.

He also possesses plenty of the outward trappings of success: a swimming pool, antiques, a motor boat, and original paintings.

But in this lawyer-executive's case, success hasn't resulted in euphoric happiness: He rated himself only fairly happy and also seems to have a quite negative attitude toward his chosen field. "The practice of law is an overcrowded and declining profession, marred by ineptitude, decaying standards, and greed," he declared.

This man has a good deal of company in his ambivalent feelings about the significance of his achievements. Nearly half of those who responded to our survey rated themselves only fairly happy with their lives. And only about half were really satisfied with specifics in their lives such as their spouses, standard of living, families, or jobs.

THE FINANCE COMPANY OFFICER

On a somewhat more upbeat note, a recently retired vice president-treasurer of a major finance company in the Northeast told us, "Success is a personal thing. It means something special and unique to all of us. To me, people at large would be happier, wiser, wealthier, and more content if they would:

1. Learn that half full means the same as half empty;
2. Use the expressions I am sorry, You may be right, and I love you! more frequently in life."

As his positive attitude suggests, this man told us he was very happy in general about his life. Furthermore, on a satisfaction scale running from zero to 10, he placed himself at the 10 level for his family life, his relationship with his spouse, and his job.

In contrast, only 58 percent of the successful people in our survey rated their relationship with their spouses in the 9 and 10 categories. Also, only 51 percent put themselves at the top of the satisfaction scale for their family life; and a surprisingly low 48 percent felt the highest levels of satisfaction for the work they do.

Still, for all his happiness and satisfaction, this man didn't present us with a picture of total fulfillment. He said rather wistfully, "I always felt I could have been a good CEO of our company."

He also indicated that he never had any clear goals for his career. And when asked whether or not he would embark on the same career again, he said he had no opinion. So even though he is an apparently happy and successful man, he is also bothered by might-have-beens.

THE PROFESSOR

The quality of family life can have a decided impact on how much successful people enjoy their success. In fact, many times individuals may define success, at least partly, in terms of how well they are serving others and how their relationships with spouse and children are going.

One professor at a major university said that he regarded "being able to contribute to society" as the most important factor in success. And he felt that he had come close to maximizing his contribution to society in his life and career.

But things were not so upbeat on the family front. He indicated that, during his first marriage, he had been highly satisfied with his personal life, his spouse, the way he enjoyed his free time, and his standard of living. But when he remarried, his level of satisfaction in all these areas dropped dramatically. He rated himself as very happy during his first marriage and just fairly happy during his second.

Despite these flaws in the fabric of his achievement, this man is a prototype of the successful, modern-day Renaissance man. He rated himself A+ in self-confidence, self-reliance, conversational ability, ability to get things done, general intelligence, common sense, specialized knowledge required in his field, and leadership ability. And there was good reason for his lofty view of himself: He had innate drive and self-confidence to move to the top in more than one occupational field.

"I've had success in several different fields, with my [multifaceted] professional training," he explained. "There's been the government, church, nonprofit work, university administration, and teaching. But all have had a commonality of service opportunity. They have required personal caring, sensitivity, analytical skills, organizational skills, leadership, conceptualization, concrete application, a holistic overview, and the need to learn a new set of specifics."

And behind all the career success was a stable, rewarding family life: "I was blessed with an exceptional marriage and children who have become fine adults and parents. In fact, this family success mothered many of the ingredients involved in career success."

This man, who makes less than $50,000 a year and has relatively few of the material trappings of success, has consciously chosen interesting or socially useful work over the rewards of big pay or high status. In contrast, more than four out of five of the top achievers we surveyed made more than $50,000 a year, and nearly two in five earned in excess of $100,000 annually. So clearly, this man wasn't representative of his more affluent, successful peers.

Still, he notes, "I have greatly enjoyed the fruits of success. But several times, I've taken lower pay and status where intrinsic satisfaction and service opportunities beckoned—and they were the right moves every time."

He also offers a personal definition of success that rejects the materialism often associated with high levels of achievement.

"Success is:

1. *Dynamic,* not static. It is always temporary, but constantly renewable.
2. What you contribute, not what you take.
3. Wonderful when shared, flat by itself.
4. Internal and not to be measured by what gets one into *Who's Who.*"

It's interesting to compare this professor's observations with another success survey we took of the general American public. Most people who responded were not at the top level of success by most definitions. So predictably, their views of

14

success diverge considerably from the lives and attitudes of those who actually have attained significant success.

For example, we asked the general public, "In your opinion, how much income per year does a person need to be considered a success in America today?"

The median income in their answers was $37,000—or considerably less than what the large majority of our *Who's Who* group is making. (See Figure 1–2.)

Also, we asked those participating in this survey of the general public to consider, from a list of 12 factors, the three that they considered most important as criteria for judging personal success. The most important indications of success, in order of frequency mentioned, were:

- Good health—58 percent
- An enjoyable job—49 percent
- A happy family—45 percent
- A good education—39 percent
- Peace of mind—34 percent
- Good friends—25 percent
- Such materialistic factors as unlimited money, a luxury car, and an expensive home brought up the rear.

Defining success, then, whether it's done by those who already are successful or those who haven't quite made it, is a rather complicated affair. Clearly, there are outward trappings and recognition factors. But, as we've seen, there is an inner dimension as well. To be successful, one must in some way *feel* successful. There must be a sense of having "arrived" or of having achieved long-range objectives or goals.

Perhaps the first step should be for you to mull over some of these points about the basic meaning of success and then to come up with your own personal definition. To this

Figure 1-2
ANNUAL INCOME OF SURVEY RESPONDENTS

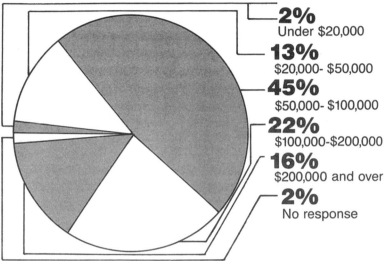

2%
Under $20,000

13%
$20,000- $50,000

45%
$50,000- $100,000

22%
$100,000-$200,000

16%
$200,000 and over

2%
No response

end, it might help to ask yourself a few questions. For example:

Where do you want to be when you reach age 65 or 70? What ultimate achievement or state of being would give you the most satisfaction in life? What values in life are most important to you—and what can you do to live out those values in a complete and meaningful way?

Two out of three of the successful people we polled said that they had always had pretty clear goals both for their careers and for their lives. Also, one in three acknowledged that definite goal setting had been extremely important for his or her own success.

In almost every case, those who do set goals and formulate strategies to achieve them find they are better off for having done so. Perhaps it's because they become more conscious of the process by which high achievement occurs. This understanding may enable them to position themselves to reach the top in their chosen field.

In the same way, we want to help you understand more about how success happens—and to assist you to become a high achiever by formulating some clear-cut strategies for your personal success. Specifically, in the following pages we'll be discussing:

- The influence your family background could have on your potential for high achievement.
- The probable impact of your educational background on your chances for success.
- Whether there's a "successful personality"—a type of person who just naturally becomes a winner in life.
- The role of luck and timing in super success.
- Whether religion is important in achieving success.
- The exact nature of the rewards that successful people enjoy.
- The way top achievers use their time.
- How the most successful people in America view the opportunities of tomorrow.
- Your personal "success quotient"—a test to show you what your chances for success are.

CHAPTER

THE FAMILY FACTORS

The main factor was my good fortune in having parents rich enough to afford (a) a good piano teacher and (b) a good (i.e., private school and good university) education. The second factor was an innate talent for music and lyrics, but [this second factor] would most probably not have been transmuted into "success" without the first factor.

Tom Lehrer, writer of humorous songs

Television entertainer Ed McMahon says his father impressed him at an early age with a favorite saying: "Always walk in a place like you belong—and most people will believe you do!"

Hard as it is to believe as you watch McMahon's apparent self-assurance and strong presence on the "Tonight Show" and other network programs, he had trouble relating to other youngsters when he was a schoolboy.

"I went to 15 different schools before I finished high school," he explains. "You see, my father was a fundraiser, and we were constantly traveling. Consequently, I would be in a school where no one knew me—and that was a tough situation. You know how cruel people can be to strangers."

One problem was that he would develop a regional accent while he was living in one part of the country. Then, he'd move to another state and discover that he "talked funny."

"You know, one year I'd be in New York with a Massachu-setts accent, and then the next year, I'd be in Massachusetts with a New York accent," he said. "So I was called various things by various kids—'Hey, New Jersey!', 'Look out, Phila-delphia!', whatever."

Although there was constant pressure from his peers to make him feel like an outsider, McMahon refused to succumb. He hung on to his father's advice for dear life. No matter how unfamiliar or uncomfortable a situation, he says, "I always tried to look like I was supposed to be there."

And it worked. "I moved from a naturally shy, wallflower type to being very aggressive. I really got on top of things."

The power of that single bit of advice from his father emerged clearly in McMahon's increasing ability to influence and lead other people. When he entered college, he became president of his freshman class.

In McMahon's case, the father offered sound advice and then allowed his son the room to apply it in his own way. And this TV star isn't by any means an isolated example of the beneficial impact of this low-key but still quite powerful form of parental influence. Other achievers we've interviewed offer a similar testimony about how their family backgrounds helped them.

Specifically, a number of the nation's most successful people say that sometimes the best way parents can encourage success in their children is to be supportive—but to provide that support more as a backdrop than through active intervention and control in the child's life. Many youngsters can really blossom under these circumstances since they are allowed plenty of freedom to develop innate skills and interests.

To illustrate this point further, let's shift the scene to a small southern town in the early part of this century. The characters are two preteen children, their mother, and their father. And the atmosphere is *definitely* laissez-faire.

The result in this case—an actual situation we came across —was two children who turned out to be super achievers. One of them, now a prominent writer, emphasized that her mother, the primary parental caretaker, had a hands-off policy toward the upbringing of both her and her younger brother. The mother gave top priority to allowing the two kids great freedom and solid encouragement in developing their special skills and interests.

"From the beginning, I was writing—even before I could spell too well," she said. "My brother [who later became an accomplished scientist] kept the drawers in his room full of mechanical gadgets—and his clothes on chairs. I kept my drawers full of papers—and my clothes on chairs. *Mother never interfered!*"

Even when the family was ready to sit down to eat, the intellectual interests of the children took precedence. "Mother had another understanding about my writing," this woman explained. "When I had an idea and got involved in it, she didn't call me to dinner. She just explained that 'Sandy got hungry and ate early.' She didn't clear the table but left that for me to do when I came up for air. Then, I ate, cleared the table, and that was that."

As if to explain the success of this parental free rein, this woman stressed in one answer to us, "My family on both sides were artistically talented." In other words, if the genes—the innate talents—are there, then a fertile soil of supportive freedom will cause them to burst forth in full bloom.

Whatever the reasons, the experiences of both Ed McMahon and this southern writer indicate how important family influence can be in a person's success. Of course, exactly how that influence works out in any given case isn't always predictable. But our survey of prominent Americans did reveal a number of general tendencies about the impact of family life on future achievement.

For example, the high achievers ranked material advan-

21

tages, such as money and property, as having little or no influence on their later achievements in life. One quarter rated material advantages at the lowest end of a scale of zero to 10; three fourths put material advantages in the middle—almost no one put this factor at the top.

So toss out any silver spoon theory of success!

Another family factor that didn't rate very highly with our successful people was national ancestry. Proud as a person may be about a particular ethnic or cultural heritage, only 10 percent of those we surveyed gave this factor a 9 or 10 rating. Slightly more than half valued this factor as mildly important, and 30 percent assigned it little or no importance in their success.

Also, the old adage that success depends not on what you know but on whom you know apparently doesn't apply to family contacts—at least not as far as our respondents are concerned. Again, only 12 percent gave this factor a top rating as an ingredient in their accomplishments.

So what *was* important about family background?

The super achievers we surveyed thought that the strongest family factor for future success was, without question, a happy home life. One half of our group ranked it as a very strong element, with one third giving this factor a top-notch 9 or 10 rating. Another 4 out of 10 regarded it as somewhat important, and fewer than 1 in 10 saw happiness at home as having little or no importance.

Other family factors that ranked near the top for our high achievers were: the strong support of parents, strong support by other family members, and physical environment or habitat when the person was young. (See Figure 2–1.)

Thus, a pattern begins to emerge. The seeds of success, it would seem, are sown not in the soil of riches, but in the good earth of love, understanding, and a nurturing home life.

But there was one peculiar blip in the responses we re-

Figure 2-1
FAMILY ENVIRONMENT & INFLUENCE   (9 or 10 Rating)

Happiness of home life	**33%**
Strong support of parents	**31%**
Strong support of family members	**28%**
Physical environment or habitat when young	**23%**
Strong religious upbringing	**16%**
Important personal contacts	**12%**
National ancestry, parents' ancestry, nationality	**11%**

ceived about the impact of family life—and that concerns the significance of religion. We asked whether a strong religious upbringing contributed to future success. We got a decided split in opinion. About one fourth said religion hadn't mattered at all in their families, but 16 percent said it mattered very much! The rest of those we polled were more lukewarm about the subject.

To better understand the specific ways that some of these family factors can provide a foundation for success, let's turn to some concrete examples from our research. In particular, we'll examine in greater depth four of the factors that we've been considering—happiness at home, physical environment, parental support, and religious upbringing. Each of these illustrates how even seemingly tenuous threads of influence at an early age can make a big difference in the final fabric of success.

THE HAPPINESS FACTOR

In addition to asking the successful people we polled to rate the happiness of their home life on a scale of zero to 10, we also asked them this question: "How happy a childhood did you have—very happy, fairly happy, fairly unhappy, very unhappy?"

Only 1 percent said they were very unhappy, and 12 percent placed themselves in the fairly unhappy category. In contrast, more than half called themselves fairly happy, and one third said they were very happy.

One top-level corporate personnel officer from the Northeast rated the happiness of his home life at the top of one of our scales. He emphasized that he got along particularly well with his mother, a fact that puts him in the mainstream of the answers we received from our *Who's Who* sample.

Specifically, 64 percent of the successful people who responded to our survey said they got along very well with their mothers. And 46 percent got along very well with their fathers. As a matter of fact, the overwhelming majority, or more than 8 out of 10, got along either very well or at least fairly well with their fathers. Even more, 9 out of 10, got along very well or fairly well with their mothers.

Our personnel officer, who hit it off especially well with his mother, had an excellent record in school. So he had plenty of intellectual horsepower—a factor that undoubtedly helped him to rise to the top of his field and earn nearly $100,000 in compensation.

But brains were only part of the reason for his success. Just as important, it would seem, was a family life that taught him how to achieve and be happy, even in the face of hardship. As he tells it, "I'm a Depression person. I grew up in a farming community, and my father was unemployed for years."

But he also noted that he is a quick learner and that he

made a major effort to work hard, in part because it was very important to his parents that he got good grades.

So, with this background, he wended his way through several sets of goals, educational experiences, and jobs: "I wanted to be a chemical engineer and was reputed to be a good one. Then, I graduated from law school at night after World War II. Finally, I wandered into personnel work, my life work."

And a few decades later, this personnel officer became a nationally known expert in his field. "Like the bear, I always wanted to see the other side of the mountain," he notes. "Who? Where? When? Why? How? What are the alternatives?"

And there's a continuity between the beneficial family experiences of his childhood and his family life as an adult. Now, he says, "I've been blessed with a marvelous wife who shares my roots—hometown, Protestant, Germanic origins, love of people."

To sum up, he declares, "I wouldn't change much if I had it to do over. I still try to follow my Christian teachings, and I have a lot to pay back to others."

This man's story suggests that happiness in childhood isn't a simple thing to define. It means different things to different people. In fact, although some sort of happiness during the early years characterizes most of the successful people we encountered, no one need feel that childhood bliss is a sine qua non of success.

Consider, for instance, the case of a prominent attorney from the Southwest who indicated that he had experienced a very unhappy childhood. That fact placed him in the bottom 1 percent of those we interviewed about this subject. But still, he is at the top of his field, he makes close to a six-figure income, and he considers himself very happy now.

When asked how he had gotten along with his mother and father, he replied "not at all" in both cases. They were apparently rather hard on him as he was growing up, especially as far as his academic performance was concerned. Good grades were very important to his parents, and they punished him for poor grades.

In part, this parental pressure may have come from the fact that his father and mother were self-made people, starting out in life quite poor. But over time, through dint of hard work and sacrifice, they became wealthy. It seems that they may have projected their need to achieve onto their son in a way that made his early life unpleasant.

But there is a happy ending to this story. Although this attorney indicated that approval by his parents wasn't important to him in his career, he rated their approval of him at the 10 level.

The negative experiences this man had in his early family life have had one major benefit for him: He has developed an effective and comprehensive philosophy of parenting, which he has put into practice with his own family. As a result, he now is extremely satisfied about his relationships with his wife and children.

He describes his philosophy of parenthood this way: "Our society appears to have failed to develop an effective and enduring mechanism to communicate sound values and life wisdom from the older generation to the younger.

"For example, there is no in-place mechanism for transmitting parenting skills and knowledge. As a result, each generation commits the errors of the past. The stable family unit no longer fulfills the function, and the extended family is generally a relic of the past. We segregate our oldest citizens and thus exacerbate the problem.

"The lack of continuity results in rapid (by historical standards) swings in values and goals, thus increasing the stress of rapid technological and economic change. Perhaps the challenge could be met by our educational system—but only if we recognize that teaching and education are sufficiently important to reward that profession economically at the level consonant with the social role to be fulfilled."

So even though happiness in childhood is usually essential to later success, a person with plenty of drive and intelligence certainly shouldn't despair. There are plenty of routes to the top, even if one's early life has been something of a disaster.

THE PHYSICAL ENVIRONMENT FACTOR

A child's physical environment doesn't necessarily have to be a bed of roses. Often, it's helpful for children to deal with challenge and struggle—with parental support and encouragement.

TV sports commentator Howard Cosell faced some tough challenges as a poor, Jewish youngster growing up in a predominantly Catholic neighborhood in Brooklyn.

"My family never had any money, and there was always economic insecurity in the household," he said. "Yet they managed to send me to college. And I always searched for economic security for myself and my family as a result of that upbringing."

Feeling a lack of security, then, made Cosell strive harder for success later in life. And he also learned the all-important quality of resilience, as he bounced back from rejections and difficulties in that sometimes hostile early environment.

"As a Jewish kid, growing up in Brooklyn right near St. Teresa's Parish, I faced attacks by a certain small coterie of Catholic kids," he recalled.

"Anti-Semitic attacks?" he was asked.

"Yes."

"And how did you respond?"

"I climbed over a back fence and ran to get to my high school," he said. "I avoided them. Later on, when I was a major in the army and still in Brooklyn, I'd run into them, but this time, they'd step to and salute. Where they once had seemed huge to me as a little kid, now they appeared to be midgets. And I wondered how I could ever have been frightened of them. But that's part of growing up in a heterogeneous society."

In effect, Cosell learned not to butt his head up against impossible situations in his difficult childhood environment but rather to execute an end run around them. But he also indicated that he would never execute that end run at the expense of his own integrity.

From the very beginning, he learned "you've got to believe in what you do and have the integrity, principles, and brains to execute that belief. I'm incapable of being a fraud. I tell it like it is."

Another accomplished man, who also faced some early struggles in an essentially positive family environment, became an award-winning research chemist. Although he now makes more than $100,000 a year, this scientist came out of a large, poor, one-parent family and faced some early childhood struggles.

(Most of our highly successful respondents came from smaller families. Specifically, 16 percent were only children; 33 percent came from two-child families; 24 percent from families with three children; and 10 percent from four-child situations. Only 11 percent of those who responded were, like this chemist, members of families with five or more youngsters.)

But still, this man rated his physical environment as being extremely important to his later success: He gave it a perfect 10.

What caused him to feel this way?

"I was raised a Christian Scientist, which teaches that anything is possible. The impossibility of this religion was superimposed on an ebullient, vigorous, and optimistic temperament and a skeptical intellect. The resulting interplay has been highly profitable."

He goes on to point out several factors in his early life that he feels were particularly important to his later adult drive and success: "My father, a lawyer, died, when I was four-years old—the only boy in a family of four sisters and a mother. This freed me to assemble my own father image, which was not completed until I was about 40 years old.

"My mother taught me ambition, the love of books and ideas, music, and sport.

"Circumstances and many early jobs taught me discipline and the rewards for hard work.

"Books gave me contact with the great minds of history— quite a bridge from a Vermont home to 4,000 years of history and cultural evolution.

"Also, we moved a lot, and that required many adjustments. I was taught constantly by bad examples, and I learned that education, discipline, single-mindedness, planning, and vigor are innately virtuous. I also learned early that joining others helps everyone.

"My greatest strengths are high imaginative potential, careful judgment of all options, and an ability to turn dreams into reality. I'm also fairly enterprising, adaptable, nondoctrinaire, and pragmatic. Underlying everything else is my good mental and physical health."

This chemist has completely rejected his early religious influences. In fact, he lists no religious preference and gives the lowest rating, zero, to questions asking whether or not he has a close personal relationship with God, believes that God has a plan for his life, or even believes in a supreme being.

At the same time, he obviously regards as quite beneficial his struggle to reconcile the positive-thinking religious influence that pervaded his early home life with his own active, questioning intellect. The result of this tension was a can-do attitude that enhanced his chances for success.

Finally, the aspect of his physical environment that apparently had the greatest impact was the books his mother provided for him. Even though his family had little money for reading matter or anything else, he says he read *much* more than his peers during grammar school, high school, and college. Also, he still continues to read about 20 books a year, and they tend to be heavy tomes. His current project is Gibbon's *Decline and Fall of the Roman Empire.*

In this same vein, he advises young people who want to succeed to "study the lives of people they admire and emulate those traits that appear attractive and valuable. Work hard toward specific goals, develop a useful imagination, and learn to inspire others."

This chemist was most influenced by his teachers and the heroes in books that constantly surrounded him in his home. And the models he found in his reading and academic interests continue to motivate him to even greater heights. Though now in his mid-60s, he is still forging ahead toward his next goals—to win a Nobel prize and to write a novel!

THE PARENTAL SUPPORT FACTOR

When Willard Scott, the weatherman on NBC's "The Today Show," was a youngster, his mother, Thelma, used to read him *The Little Engine That Could.* Using the little locomotive in the story as an example, she would tell him he could be anything he wanted to be. Scott's father, Herman, encouraged his son's teenage forays into radio work and his other childhood enthusiasms.

In his *Joy of Living,* Scott sums up the impact of his parents on his later success:

"I had what every kid wants and needs: parents who let me know that I was a VIP in their lives. I had Herman, who took me places and talked to me and put himself out for me. And I had Thelma, who literally bathed me in love."

Charles Schwab, the founder of the world's largest discount brokerage house, had a similar experience as a youngster. He was always oriented toward entrepreneurial ventures, and his parents were ready and willing to open their home and backyard to practically anything he wanted to try.

So, he started out by picking up walnuts around the neighborhood, putting them into sacks, and storing them at his house until he had enough to sell. Then, at age 12, he graduated to running a small chicken operation—once again, with his parent's complete approval. He had a dozen chicks by the time he was 13 and soon developed what he calls "a fully integrated operation" by offering eggs, fryers, and chicken fertilizer.

This may be the ultimate example of love and support from parents—to put up not only with chickens but even with their fertilizer!

The experiences of Scott and Schwab coincide with those of many other successful people. When we asked our top achievers what childhood family factors had contributed to their adult success, nearly one third gave the highest marks—a 9 or 10—to strong support of parents. And that's the way a leading professor from Ohio responded about his mother and father, who had been born abroad.

"My parents were first-generation immigrants from Europe," he said. "They stressed—besides health, cleanliness, and common domestic virtues—the importance of education, of opportunity, of personal well-being, of independence, and of progress. In short, they stressed being better and happier people than our own immediate ancestors."

In this man's case, however, parental support didn't go hand in hand with a supremely happy home life. He said he had a *fairly* happy childhood and got along fairly well with both his mother and father.

Because there were three other children in the family and the family was poor, the parents undoubtedly had to limit the amount of time they could spend with any one child. So this man may not have received an overabundance of attention from one or both of his parents. But they were strict and attentive toward him as far as his schoolwork was concerned: He was rewarded for good grades and punished for poor ones.

Even with the limitations that he and his parents faced adjusting to a new country, the parental influence on this professor certainly seemed to "take" as far as his career was concerned. From his responses to our survey, it's evident that he emulated:

- Their dedication to hard work.
- Their commitment to education.
- Their ambition.
- Their ability to get things done.

He summed it all up nicely when we asked him to give us his formula for success: "Having first-rate teachers [and other examples] who were distinguished not only by their discipline but also by their humane concern for disciples. Then, seeking to imitate these masterpieces in one's life with imagination, independence, common sense, and hard work."

THE FAMILY RELIGION FACTOR

One of those who listed a strong religious upbringing as important to his future success (a perfect 10) was a prominent professor who had grown up as the son of missionaries to

China. He also said his childhood was a very happy experience.

"I was in a British boarding school from ages 9 to 16," he says. "Although my citizenship is in the United States, I consider my background sufficient to call myself a cosmopolite rather than a Texan or American in the narrow sense."

This worldwide perspective, which has been nurtured since early childhood, has made him extremely sensitive to international affairs and problems. "I do have a strong feeling of nationhood," he explained. "And I feel that America has the leadership of the world as its charge. But we have yet to acknowledge that position, much less to forge a national and international policy that we can afford and that the rest of the free world will feel comfortable with."

Interestingly, although he had a very happy childhood, this man says he got along just fairly well with his mother and father. Also, although he always had clear goals for his life and career, he says that his parents only had a mild influence on these goals. A high school teacher had the most influence on his goal setting.

There are a number of possible reasons for the limited impact of this man's family on his goals. For example, as the youngest of five children and a boarding school student, he may have spent less time with his parents than children in smaller families.

But it's also clear that as far as religious faith is concerned, his parents made a big impression on him. In short, this may be a case where the quality rather than the quantity of parenting time was the most important factor. Indeed, there can be little question that the values of the parents were passed on to the child. Thus, in outlining his formula for success in his field, he listed, "integrity, high goals, and knowing the will of God."

As further evidence of the strong influence he has continued to feel from his family religion and traditional values, this professor said that the Bible was a book that had the greatest impact on his life. And the book he was currently reading was C. S. Lewis' *Mere Christianity.*

So family religion does make a difference. But it doesn't always make the kind of difference you might expect.

These, then, are a few indications of what an important impact a person's home life can have on later success. But it's important to avoid being simplistic. As we've seen in some of the illustrations, not everybody enjoyed unmitigated happiness at home, support of parents, or satisfaction with the childhood environment.

But even with the limitations and pressures in any given home—or the shortcomings of any particular set of parents— the childhood years are a time for putting down the roots that will give rise to later success. Our study shows that, although it's not essential, it's certainly very helpful for a child to grow up in a happy home with the strong support of parents and other family members.

Obviously, there's nothing you can do now to change your childhood. But you can rise above any deficiencies, as did many of the successful people we studied.

CHAPTER

SCHOOLED FOR SUCCESS

Apart from being well trained and professionaly competent in the field in which one works, is the need for keen curiosity about everything and anything related to it.

Jonas Salk, Medical Researchcr

When he was a high school student, newscaster Morton Dean learned a great deal about dealing with the disconcerting surprises of life.

"I did a lot of bench time as a high school football player," he recalls. "And I remember suddenly being called off the bench during one game when my team was a yard and a half from the goal line. I was a reserve quarterback and hadn't played yet that season. But we used a very simple, basic offense, and I think the coach thought this was a good chance for me to go in. He wanted me to achieve something so that I could build up my confidence.

"So he said, 'Throw a jump pass.'

"For us, that goal-line play just meant stepping back, jumping up, and popping the ball to the end. It would have been a touchdown—on my very first play.

But what did Dean actually do?

"I ran in, got the ball, fumbled it, and fell on it. I've had nightmares about this ever since. My father always said, *ad nauseum,* 'You've got to be prepared to come off the bench.' But that day, I wasn't prepared."

Ever since that experience, Dean has always tried to be ready for any surprise. "In the television news business, a lot of people try to pretend that they just come on without any preparation and do it perfectly," he says. "But it doesn't work that way. You have to do your homework. It ain't that easy."

Do your homework. Prepare for the unexpected. Learn all you can before you plunge into a job. That's the lesson Dean learned during his school days. And it's also something other highly successful people learned from their academic experiences.

One of the top achievers we interviewed, a professor at a major Southwestern university, also is a proponent of preparation—especially in formal classwork: "When I was five years old and was asked what I wanted to be when I grew up, I replied, 'I don't care as long as I can learn and learn and learn!' "

And she goes on to say, "I have done just that."

Indeed she has, having graduated fourth in a high school class of 400. Various teachers motivated her strongly during those years, and math and music were her favorite subjects.

But her school interests weren't limited to the classroom. She found time for the band, orchestra, choir, French club, math club, and chess club. In addition, she participated in the Girl Scouts, took a life-saving course, and worked part time.

This woman's aggressive approach to achievement and

participation in a wide variety of activities continued into her college years. She pursued her interest in mathematics and music, with a special interest in the organ. She also worked her way through college.

The result, once again, was success: She graduated in the top 2 percent of her class. Then she went on to graduate school—first medical school, then law school. In fact, she made it through 25 years of school in all!

Now, she holds down a major professorship, earns a good salary, and enjoys satisfying relationships with her husband and children. Interestingly, she says she's experienced little or no sex discrimination in her career. In part, this was probably because she's a bright, competent person; and in part, she says, it's because her field of endeavor—interdisciplinary work in health and the law—is so unique.

Her future goals? They're quite consistent with her life's philosophy: "To continue to learn as long as I live."

Too often, the public has not viewed learning for its own sake as an important key to success. Even worse, people usually picture scholars in the humanities and other "nonpractical" fields as bookworms, grinds, or nerds—absent-minded bumblers oblivious of the real world.

To be sure, there are some practical, dollars-and-cents reasons for these negative attitudes toward a broad education. According to a 1982 study, for example, young people entering college today tend to take courses that will provide them with immediate practical skills. This study, conducted by the American Council on Education for the National Science Foundation and the National Endowment for the Humanities, showed that the top high school graduates were increasingly enrolling in engineering and science programs. (For purposes of the study, top students were those with the highest scores on their SATs.) What was the primary attraction of these two fields? Word is out that that's where the big bucks can be made.

But even though many of the most ambitious students

are migrating away from the traditional liberal arts degrees, our findings suggest they could be making a mistake. In fact, one theme kept recurring as the nation's top achievers discussed their educational experiences: *it's important to learn as much as possible about as many things as possible.*

A few of these super successes gave the following advice:

- A research scientist and inventor with an income in the six-figure range had this advice for young people: "In college, take all the most difficult, fundamental courses so as to have a broad base of understanding."
- The director of a symphony orchestra stated that he believes in the virtue of acquiring a broad educational background.
- An artist, when asked what advice he would give to young people entering his field, responded, "It is not what you may learn that will harm you, but rather what you have *not* learned."

Many successful people also feel it's important not to narrow your options to one specialty too soon. Rather, it's better to stay open and learn as much as possible until you are certain of your talents and interests. Even our high achievers who had specific career goals from the time they were children often advised younger people to get as broad a background and as much training as possible.

But now, let's get more specific about how the educational experience can contribute to an individual's success. In one part of our survey, under the heading "Factors Contributing To Success," we asked the nation's most successful people to rank various aspects in their academic experience on a scale of zero to 10. In other words, they would circle zero if a school-oriented factor was totally unimportant to their personal success in their chosen field. And they would circle 10 if it was of the highest importance.

Here's a percentage breakdown of those who assigned the greatest importance—a rating of 9 or 10—to each of the factors listed.

Academic experience	*Percent who gave a 9 or 10 rating to academics as a highly important factor that contributed to their success*
Desire to excel	58%
Good work habits, ability to organize time, get things done	53
Having natural learning ability	46
Working hard at schoolwork	42
Getting good grades	32
Attending high-quality school(s)	31
Influence and encouragement of teachers	31
Having specific academic goals	26
Scoring well on achievement tests	25
Involvement in extracurricular activities	16
Involvement in sports	5

As you see from this survey, these high achievers considered the desire to excel the most important success-producing factor in their academic experience. But how exactly can this quality lead to future achievements in the working world?

The obvious way is that in an occupation, as in academe,

Figure 3-1
ACADEMIC EXPERIENCE   (9 or 10 Rating)

Category	Rating
Desire to excel	58%
Good work habits, organize time, get things done	53%
Having natural learning ability	46%
Working hard at school work	42%
Getting good grades	32%
Attending high-quality school(s)	31%
Influence & encouragement of teachers	31%
Having specific academic goals	26%

you can't be afraid to compete if you want to be a success. Any fear of failure that you might be harboring or any impulse to stay lost in the crowd must be overcome and conquered.

Next in importance to excelling was the development of good work habits in school. This means learning how to be a self-starter. You have to get started, stick with it, and get finished on time.

The following two success-related factors were closely ranked on our rating list: The top achievers listed natural learning ability next and, just below it, the importance of hard work. One inference is that these two factors should go hand in hand if you want to have the best chance to succeed in life. That is, it would be unwise to rely too heavily on natural ability without working hard to improve whatever talent you possess.

But how about getting a broad educational background?

This principle seems to be implied at several points in the figures. For example, if one attends a high-quality school—

which one third of our respondents said was important—that person will probably get a broad, high-quality liberal arts education.

Also notice that having specific academic goals was given a fairly low rating. This may mean, at least in part: Don't narrow your sights too soon! In other words, young people should give themselves the time and opportunity to discover their interests and talents by exploring a variety of subjects.

Another scholarly characteristic that fits in with high achievement in life is a love of reading. And predictably, the vast majority of successful people read many more books than the average person. For most of them, reading as a pastime began early in life. Almost three quarters of our achievers reported that they read more (independently of any school assignments) than other kids their age when they were 10 years old or younger.

Apparently, reading is a pursuit that lasts a lifetime for the majority of top achievers. In fact, about the same proportion of successful people who were currently reading a book when they responded to our survey—3 out of 4—also read more than their peers at 10 years of age and continued to do so throughout their school years.

Of course, being an avid reader won't automatically make you a success; but it's clearly a trait that many successful people have in common. For many of the achievers we interviewed, it was an important early step on the road to their later success as adults.

Finally, school days were important for our high achievers in at least four other key ways:

- *Mentors began to emerge:* Nearly 9 out of 10 said they had one or more teachers who made them enthusiastic about a particular subject.
- *A tendency to specialize became evident:* Two thirds said their grades tended to be better in some courses than in others.

41

- *Parents got involved in the education process:* Nearly 9 in 10 said that it was of some importance to their parents that they got good grades.
- *In most cases, parents were nonjudgmental about performance:* Less than a quarter said they had been rewarded in some way for good grades, and fewer than 1 in 10 said they were punished for poor marks.

So these are some of the broad academic brush strokes that help create the early outlines of success. But now, let's move from general trends to specifics, as we examine the role that school played for some individuals. We like to think of these experiences as illustrating certain lessons about the important role that an academic background may play in success.

LESSON 1: Develop Work Habits in School that Turn You into a Self-Starter

Successful people don't usually have someone standing over them, driving them toward peaks of achievement. Rather, they tend to be self-starters. And most often, this characteristic begins to appear and be nurtured during the early academic experience.

John Templeton, regarded by many as one of the greatest investors and mutual fund managers of all time, says that he learned some basic principles of self-starting during his grammar school days in the backwoods of Tennessee. His father first provided the impetus by giving him a challenge: If John got a report with nothing but As on it, he'd get a bale of cotton. But if he didn't have straight As, he'd have to give his father a bale of cotton.

When the final tally was in after 11 years of schooling, John had 22 bales of cotton, one for every semester of school. And his father had none!

Of course, Templeton didn't just respond to material rewards in his studies. He used to sit in the front row of his classes, right under the teacher's nose, because he wanted to learn and didn't want to miss a trick while the teacher was talking.

His tendency to take the initiative intensified as he got older. He decided on his own that he wanted to go to college at Yale, even though practically nobody in his little Tennessee town knew a thing about the Ivy League. So each year in high school, he arranged to take a series of entrance exams miles away at Vanderbilt University.

As a result of all this independent effort, Templeton got into Yale, went through four years on a scholarship, and graduated Phi Beta Kappa. With this record of achievement behind him—and also the independent, self-starting work habits that he developed—he began to succeed in short order in the investment world.

Now a multimillionaire who personally funds the $200,000 a year Templeton Prize for Progress in Religion, he lives in a palatial mansion in the Bahamas. But it's doubtful whether any of this would have been possible without his ability to take the initiative, which he had developed from his early school years.[1]

A somewhat different picture—but with the same basic call to independent initiative in school—is presented by a state supreme court judge.

First of all, tongue in cheek, he wrote: "Someone once said that a judge's success can be attributed to three things: (1) a beautiful head of white hair to appear distinguished; (2) a good case of hemorrhoids to appear to be concerned; and (3) a good bladder for long sittings."

---

[1] For an expanded version of Templeton's story, see William Proctor's *The Templeton Touch* (Garden City, N.Y.: Doubleday Publishing, 1983).

Yet that certainly doesn't say it all about this judge. At the top of his list of important factors leading to success are several that relate directly to a good education.

For one thing, he places the highest value on learning to work hard in school as a factor contributing to his own success. Equally important in his mind was getting academic tasks organized and completed.

This judge also believes that developing diligence and good work habits, along with a desire to excel and a natural ability to learn, was more important to his later success than the quality of the school he attended.

For this man, school was mainly a training ground in strengthening success-oriented traits. The academic subject matter was of secondary importance.

Extracurricular activities were also an important part of this jurist's experience. He was active in sports, debating, school plays, and English and math clubs while in high school. Although he was less involved in extracurricular activities in college because of a need to earn money, he still feels that developing a broad range of interests contributed to his success.

Since he was one of eight children and his family's financial circumstances were only average, he had to work his way through college and law school. An education was obviously very important to him as a way to improve his lot in life, and he was willing to sacrifice to obtain one.

The personal qualities this judge began to nurture in school came into full bloom after he entered the working world. So, he considers diligence and ambition in his legal career to have been extremely important personal characteristics that led to his success, and he gave both qualities a maximum rank of 10. Also, he gave a top rating of 10 to good luck and the ability to follow instructions.

Overall, our judge comes across as a person who, while he was still a schoolboy, developed into an inner-directed youngster with a strong determination to make the most of himself. He says he was influenced by an older brother and sister, but he doesn't mention any teachers as being instrumental in his development.

Finally, to be sure we get his point about the importance of formal learning, he closed his remarks with a particularly strong call to nurture an I-can-do-it frame of mind: "Men and women must be motivated and disciplined to be educated to achieve. A student must be told that he is a winner, that he can learn to be a winner, that he must be a winner!"

LESSON 2: Even Artists Should Learn to Be Businesslike— if They Want to Succeed

One might expect an artist to have an unorthodox approach to education. But one painter, a Hawaiian who earns a five-figure income and owns two homes, sounds as much like a corporate executive as a creative type: He gave high marks to hard work in school, academic ambition, and a strong desire to excel as key factors that contributed to his career success.

And his scholarly performance bears him out, at least in the early years. In high school he was a high achiever, graduating among the top 10 in his class. At the college level, however, some of the more nonconformist juices began to flow, and he developed conflicts with traditional education on several grounds.

"College is a poor place for the artist to learn," he explained. "Academics are oriented to the notion of linear development in art. In contrast, the artist generally believes art is an inherent part of the psyche, just as the nose or liver is a fundamental and inherent part of the body."

Though this man began to specialize in art-oriented subjects at a young age, he feels it has been important to his success to have had a broad range of interests throughout his life. For one thing, he reads extensively. In fact, he reports reading 65 books, more than one a week, within the last year!

In addition to his reading he enjoys the outdoor life, which is available in abundance at his Hawaiian home. As with his academic interests and habits, he continues the same athletic orientation he had as a young man: His favorite sports activities are fishing, canoeing, swimming, sailing, and camping.

This artist's responses reveal a love of learning, a need for great variety in life, and a zest for constant improvement in his work. But he's also a hardheaded realist who has learned how to apply himself to attain success in an extremely difficult field.

LESSON 3: Develop an In-Depth Expertise in One Field

A zoologist who makes close to $100,000 annually told us, "My greatest advantage has been a long-time, intense interest in my field, starting at age seven or so. I was encouraged by my parents, who provided books as I needed them. My first scientific publication (in a regular technical journal) was at age 16, and I wrote more throughout my university and subsequent years."

As you might expect, this man casts an enthusiastic vote for hard work in school. Furthermore, he's a big believer in developing a desire to excel. In his view, these qualities are primary ingredients that contributed to his success.

Though this scientist knew what he wanted to do with his life from the time he was seven and focused his attention on scientific studies, he still advises young people to get the broadest possible training. "Fields change rapidly, and it is hard to predict your needs," he explains.

And he practices what he preaches as he continues his

education—even though he is almost 70 years old. Like many of his successful peers, he reads extensively. Also, despite his active involvement in major research projects, he manages to find time to do volunteer work for his political party and environmental protection groups. He also mentions traveling as one of his favorite nonwork activities.

Even with his expansive approach to education, however, this scientist's ability to plumb the depths and scale the heights of *one* primary field remains the cornerstone of his success.

LESSON 4: Academic Variety Can Be the Spice of Life

The turning point of one college president's life occurred in an academic setting—when he left public high school to attend a private academy. "It opened up a new world to me," he says. Fascination with the world of academe followed, and he ended up making a career in education.

His early education has clearly had a profound influence on his later success. So, in evaluating his present feelings of satisfaction, he awards the highest score to the way his education prepared him for his career.

His advice to young people is as open-ended as was his early education: "Be sure to explore options and avoid premature commitment," he says. "Secure a broad liberal education and acquire skills requisite to lifelong learning."

This willingness to enter into new experiences that expand his horizons has been evident all his life: "I have always been prepared to move, gain new experience, and take on new challenges. Accordingly, my career has encompassed eight different jobs."

A lifelong thirst for knowledge is typical of practically all our respondents. And most of them found their school experience rewarding and useful to their intellectual development.

But a few very successful people, such as the man whose story follows, stand out from the rest as "antischool" types.

LESSON 5: You May Learn as Much or More from People than from Books

An advertising executive, who now makes more than $200,000 a year, claims quite emphatically that his education has been meaningless to his career and his life. He had no inclination to work hard in school. In fact, he graduated at the bottom of his class in college. He says, "I'm proud of it, and I can prove it!"

As you might expect—unlike most of his fellow achievers— this executive gives a low priority to such academic virtues as good work habits, techniques to organize time, and the ability to get school projects done. Twice he mentions that education played no part in his career success.

But when we look beyond these rather feisty, negative comments, we begin to discover some basic similarities with our other respondents. For example, this ad man says his desire to excel at school and his natural ability to learn were very high. Our other top achievers also gave the heaviest weight to these qualities as factors contributing to their later success.

Then there's a fascinating series of observations in his closing remarks. "Your individual and personal ambition plus talents that you are born with and develop determine your level of success. School has little or nothing to do with it, but teachers and intelligent friends are invaluable if you are lucky enough to meet them and talk to them at the right time."

So clearly, the academic experience was important for this executive, even if the content of his courses wasn't. It was the school relationships that really mattered to him. This point becomes even more obvious when we see that he lists a high school teacher and a college teacher as the two people who had a great deal of influence on him and his goals in life.

We notice too that he enjoyed creative writing in both high school and college, especially comedy writing. He writes, "I knew more about that and was more involved than anybody else." He became a hard worker and even something of a scholar *when something interested him.*

As an adult, he gives himself high grades for his capacity to work hard and his ambition to get ahead—tendencies often present in many of our other respondents. Having a wide range of interests from school days to the present is another quality he shares with the other members of our *Who's Who* sample.

So this man may seem different from his highly successful peers on one level; basically, he's a great deal like them.

LESSON 6: Turn Learning—and Life—into an Adventure

For one research scientist, who makes a six-figure income working for a large manufacturer, life in all its phases is an adventure. He constantly steps out into unknown territory and takes action—often to help others—without worrying too much about the ultimate consequences. But he's an optimist about where his adventures in life are leading.

"A very important factor in my life has been to cast bread upon the waters," he says. "It has usually returned manyfold. But one must not cast the bread expecting it to return; that does not work!"

The adventure of life really began for this man in the academic world. He began to read at the age of four and always read more than his fellow students. He graduated number one in his high school class and number two in college.

School was always important to him, and he gives his education a top rating of 10.

This scientist's formula for success is consistent with his venturesome approach to life: "Learn all you can, try out new things. In this way you will see what no one else has seen (with your eyes and mind). You must go your own way, driven by your own thoughts and discoveries. Often you will be wrong."

And he advises young people, "In college, take all the most difficult fundamental courses so as to have a broad base of understanding. Think for and by yourself as much as possible."

His life reflects this freewheeling and sometimes risk-seeking spirit. In his spare time he enjoys reading, hiking, skiing, farming, and fixing machines. He also belongs to a musical organization and a glider club. Moreover, listening to classical music has always been a very satisfying activity for him.

Among the books that had the greatest impact on him were the biographies of Einstein, Pasteur, Steffens, and Leonardo da Vinci—men who also took on big intellectual challenges and blazed new scientific trails. In the past year he has read 12 books, 2 of which were fiction.

This scientist has many goals for the future, one being to compose music. So the horizons of his personal and intellectual exploration of the new and unknown continues!

LESSON 7: Learn to Enjoy School and You'll Probably Enjoy Life

A former music school director and symphony orchestra director, who is a consummate example of the joie de vivre that characterizes many of our top achievers, talked about his life in these terms:

"As an educator, I have to believe in the virtues of good work habits, a broad educational background, and ultimate specialized training. I also feel that people should enjoy their chosen profession—not simply make money in it. Actually, making money is probably a pretty poor reason for choosing an occupation, and lifetime income is probably *greater* for those who put service ahead of immediate personal gain."

His own life tends to support the idea that the joy of learning should culminate in the joy of working. In high school he was the class valedictorian, and he graduated first in his class from college with a 4.0 grade average. He also reveled in a wide range of interests in both high school and college, including the school newspapers, theater groups, the French club, and musical organizations.

This musician still is a man of diversified interests. He belongs to a variety of organizations, including Rotary, retired teachers' groups, a yacht club, the U.S. Coast Guard Auxiliary, the local symphony supporters, and the museum guild. Finally, though now retired, he is working on some major writing projects.

So, here we have the profile of an exuberant winner who has never worried about spreading himself too thin. He wanted to try everything, beginning in his early school years, and he was determined to enjoy it all.

LESSON 8: Go for Graduate Work

The large majority of the successful people we surveyed not only have high IQs and did extremely well in high school and college but they also completed some graduate school-work. So we have to take seriously the advice given by this prominent psychologist we interviewed:

"Get as much education in your field as you can, preferably

a doctorate," he advises young people entering his profession. "Broaden your interests and training to include more than one field."

He concludes: "Success, however defined, is the result of doing something on a regular basis. One needs to pursue education and training in some kind of continuous fashion—e.g., advanced workshops, graduate courses—so as to upgrade skills."

In other words, the main idea is to go for higher degrees. And at the same time, be prepared to stick with your academic work over a relatively long period of time. Be patient, move ahead systematically, and success will be waiting for you as you reach one new destination after the other.

Of course, the experience and advice of each of these people are tied to some extent to the fields they've chosen. It may help in the field of education and in some other professions to have multiple degrees. But that's not necessarily true of other lines of work.

Overall, however, successful people tend to have certain common key qualities and experiences in their school years. These, in turn, lead to top achievement later on. To reiterate, some of the major academic traits and experiences include:

- A desire to excel in school.
- An ability to work hard and to organize time in order to complete assignments.
- A broad educational background before and after specializing in a particular field.
- Voracious reading habits.
- High intelligence.
- The patience and commitment to do well in high school and college, to complete a course of graduate work, and to develop a lifelong plan of study.

This survey has some clear messages for individuals who want to succeed. But is there any word here for our educational institutions?

We think there is. For one thing, to some extent the educational pendulum seems to be swinging in a success-enhancing direction at the present time. Required courses in the humanities are being reinstated, thus establishing a broader base of knowledge before specialization.

Also, grading seems to be back in good standing after the pass or fail experiment of the early 70s. This should encourage students to engage in healthy competition and develop a desire to excel.

Below the college level, we've noticed an increased interest in raising the literacy level of all students. Since a love of reading is a basic characteristic of so many successful people, we hope that this educational trend continues.

Because the school years were such an important part of most of these successful people's lives, the impact of our local and national educational policies on individual achievement should not be underestimated. It seems clear that our schools and universities provide the tools with which most people build their success.

CHAPTER

IS THERE A SUCCESS PERSONALITY?

There's an old joke about a lady who asks a man on a New York City street corner: "How do I get to Carnegie Hall, please?" The reply: "Practice, lady, practice!" That pretty much says it all. But all the practice in the world still needs luck!

Artie Shaw, composer

Is there something called a *success personality?* Or, to put it another way, is there a winning combination of personality traits that will lead almost inevitably to personal, financial, professional, or artistic achievement?

You might say that for career-minded people, this is the $64,000 question. Only in this case, the answer may be worth millions.

A common belief exists that there are indeed qualities that lead some to the top of their fields, whereas others struggle along in the middle of the pack. But if this is true, exactly what *is* that secret formula for success that lies hidden in the personality? Can you cultivate these traits?

Of course, some researchers contend that a person's personality is preprogrammed before birth—that genes are destiny, no matter what. Others maintain that we are solely products of environmental factors and external circumstances. And still other theorists borrow from both lines of thought.

But we're not here to argue the sources of personality development. Instead we're intent on identifying those traits that repeatedly earmark high achievers—traits common to the successful men and women we interviewed.

This research has pinpointed 12 general traits that recur regularly among top achievers. They emerge from individuals' self-appraisals as these achievers try to describe inner strengths that have directly contributed to their success. In various personal accounts, accomplished people have also revealed how these traits have pulled them through tight spots, motivated them to success, and kept them on top of their fields for decades.

The 12 success characteristics we've identified are:

1. Common sense.
2. Special knowledge of your field.
3. Self-reliance.
4. General intelligence.
5. Ability to get things done.
6. Leadership.
7. Knowing right from wrong.
8. Creativity and inventiveness.
9. Self-confidence.
10. Oral expression.
11. Concern for others.
12. Luck.

Sometimes, these traits overlap. In other cases, they're rather difficult to define. But whatever the deficiencies of separating various traits into these categories, there's no doubt

Figure 4-1
PERSONAL CHARACTERISTICS
OR TRAITS   (9 or 10 Rating)

Trait	
Being a hard worker	**70%**
Common sense	**61%**
Not afraid to pursue new ideas, ventures, take risks	**56%**
Caring about other people	**51%**
Not afraid to be different	**44%**
Intelligence	**43%**
Ambition	**43%**

that, when taken together, they constitute the closest thing we can find to a success personality.

SUCCESS CHARACTERISTIC 1: Common Sense

Common sense is the most common quality possessed by our successful respondents. In their self-appraisals of personality traits, 79 percent awarded themselves a top score of A in this category. Also, 61 percent said that common sense was very important in contributing to their own career success.

But what exactly do we mean by common sense?

In the minds of many of our respondents, common sense is an ability to render sound, practical judgments on the everyday affairs of life.

Although common sense may be a somewhat elusive quality to capture on paper, the most widely accepted definitions imply it is basic to human nature. According to some historical studies, until the mid-1500s, common sense was thought to be the common bond of all five senses. Others have said that common sense is simply "natural reason" or "native sagacity."

Humorist Dr. Charles Jarvis insists we all have a lot of common sense because we certainly "ain't used any!" But some people have used their common sense quite well including the high-achievers we polled who see common sense as the cornerstone of their success.

One Texas oil and gas magnate said his formula for success is his "ability to lead, adapt quickly, comprehend the situation, deal with the public, and maintain inner courage."

But he also pointed out that, in his opinion, "The key ability for success is to be able to *simplify.*"

He goes on to say that this skill, although related to intelligence and analytical powers, "is nevertheless distinct. In conducting meetings, advocating an internal course of action, dealing with industry regulators and the media, the ability to reduce one's understanding of a complex problem to the simplest terms is highly important."

Some may feel that the ability to simplify difficult concepts is a sign of high intelligence. That's undoubtedly true in many situations. For example, Einstein's brilliant insights into the relationship between matter, energy, and mass were basically simple. So are the lines on the magnificent structures designed by Frank Lloyd Wright and Le Corbusier.

On the other hand, there also seems to be a common-sense quality to simplification—an ability to sweep aside those extraneous, irrelevant thoughts and ideas and get right to the core of what matters. That's what the rich Texan we just referred to was able to do.

Of course, it's also true that he has the mental horsepower to deal with the most complex of subjects. Among other things, he's a graduate of law school, has an IQ score of 156, and earns more than $200,000 a year. But still, he relies heavily on his ability to simplify. In short, he uses his common sense to outline a concise, logical, practical course of action, which his subordinates can then understand and follow.

But is common sense something a person is born with? Or can you do something to increase your personal store of this practical commodity?

The oil man's answer is that common sense can definitely be developed. In fact, he attributes his own ability to simplify and make good, practical judgments to abilities he learned during an extracurricular activity in his school days: "I learned this skill in high school and college debate competition," he says.

He explains that debate training promotes the same techniques that common sense draws on to make a systematic, logical, reasonable decision. Likewise, he was able to give himself solid ratings of 9s and 10s for organizational ability and the ability to get things done, and these certainly are qualities directly related to common sense.

Unfortunately, little emphasis is placed on common sense in our present educational system though the trait often carries more weight in the world of work. But the fact remains that common sense is a quality that's connected to success in many careers. So it's important to find a way to incorporate it into your own personality if you hope to become a mover and shaker yourself.

SUCCESS CHARACTERISTIC 2: Specialized Knowledge of Your Field

Having specialized knowledge in a chosen field is the second most common personal characteristic possessed by our top achievers, with three fourths rating themselves in the top A categories.

A good illustration of this quality is geologist Philip Oxley, president of Tenneco Oil Exploration and Production. He attributes much of his success to having once worked in the oil fields with hours of "sitting on wells and bird-dogging seismic crews."

He learned the tricks of the trade firsthand. "People who are going to be good managers need to have practical understanding of the crafts in their business," he told *U.S. News & World Report.* Today, his expertise in this field earns him a six-figure salary.

On-the-job experience has also convinced one news photographer we interviewed of the importance of acquiring specialized knowledge in his field. He says that "understanding why the equipment I use performs the way it does" is part of his formula for success.

As part of the educational process, he regularly reads books that explain motion picture techniques. Also, he's active in the National Press Photographers' Association, the National Press Photographers' Foundation, and his local city photographers' association. These professional groups provide additional sources of information that keep him innovative and current in his field.

But like most of our other high achievers, this photographer hasn't allowed his commitment to specialization to seduce him away from extra activities after work hours. In fact, he puts a high priority on community service: "I think you have to place the betterment of society, your community, and your profession as one of your goals in life. When you do that, you become more productive in general."

As part of his involvement in community work, he spends his spare time volunteering at a local museum and helping visitors at a nearby national park.

One final point about this man: He obtained specialized knowledge in his field from self-education, not from formal schooling. In fact, he had only a couple years of college and earned no formal degree.

The pursuit of excellence in a chosen field, however, doesn't necessarily result in a happier home environment. Although another journalist we interviewed rates his professional abilities well and gives himself a high mark of 9 for success in his chosen field, he's only moderately satisfied with his personal life. Also he indicated that he's relatively dissatisfied with his family life and his relationship with his spouse.

But despite the problems he's facing at home, this individual says he derives great satisfaction from his work—and that's often an important ingredient in any success story.

Many times the ability to learn one specialized line of work depends on how much you enjoy what you're doing. In fact, "being paid for what I like to do best" is one retired professor's definition of success.

This man's natural interest in geology turned into a full-time career, a "creative experience" that has continued past teaching into retirement. By working as an author, lecturer, and consultant to a major oil company, he keeps his finger on the pulse of the field. So even in retirement, he is able to earn a five-figure salary from a specialized field that continues to fascinate him.

The importance of this coupling of personal interest and special knowledge was expressed rather nicely by an executive vice president for an industrial corporation:

"Do your homework!" he advises those seeking success. "Nothing helps success more than knowing what you're doing. It reduces the risks and works like an insurance policy for your own ability. Then, be enthusiastic in whatever you do."

This formula works so well for him that he has achieved independent success in three corporations with significantly different product lines. He rates his professional success a 9, and he also considers himself quite happy and satisfied with his personal life, including his relationship with his wife and children.

But this second success characteristic, specialized knowledge, is not something a person should take for granted. It's an ongoing imperative that must mark every step of any ascent to the top. And the learning process continues, even after major peaks of achievement have been scaled.

"To achieve success, you have to want it," this corporate officer explains. "Then, you must work to keep it. Success can be deadly because having arrived can be fatal."

In short, you have to renew your knowledge and interest in your field of expertise continually if you hope to succeed over a lifetime.

SUCCESS CHARACTERISTIC 3: Self-Reliance

Top achievers rely primarily on their own resources and abilities—that's a maxim that has become etched in our thinking as we've conducted this study of the Great American Success Story. In fact, 77 percent gave themselves an A rating for self-reliance on their personal evaluations.

Ralph Waldo Emerson, perhaps the ultimate authority on the subject, describes the quality in his famous essay titled "Self-Reliance":

Trust thyself; every heart vibrates to that iron string. Accept the place that divine providence has found for you. . . . Nothing at last is sacred but the integrity of your own mind. . . . What I must do is all that concerns me, not what people think. This rule, equally arduous in actual and in intellectual life, may serve for the whole distinction between greatness and meanness.

But now, let's move from the philosophical to the practical. Many of the success characteristics we're considering in this chapter, such as the ability to get things done and self-confidence, are related to self-reliance. Self-reliance is not how you feel or how good you are; rather, it's whether you have the *courage* to take definitive action to get things moving in your life. So, as part of our definition of self-reliance, we've included (1) the ability to set goals, and (2) plain old willpower.

Now, what do our top achievers have to say about this topic? Here are their main ideas, presented in the form of some principles that promote self-reliance.

Self-Reliance Principle 1: Well-defined goals

Two thirds of the successful individuals we surveyed said they've always had pretty clear goals for their lives. Likewise, two thirds had pretty clear goals for their careers.

We also asked the question a somewhat different way and came up with a similar result. We asked respondents how well this statement described them personally: "I have well-defined personal goals." In this case, 32 percent rated themselves at the 9 or 10 level, and another 46 percent marked a relatively high 6 to 8 rating.

One quite successful person who places an extremely high value on goal setting is actress Arlene Dahl. Now an entrepreneur and author, she uses a variation on a New Year's resolution technique.

"Every year on January 1, I take a sheet of paper and an envelope, and I write down all the things I want to change in my life," she explained to us. "It may be a self-improvement program, a diet, a language course, something in my businesses—whatever I feel I need to do during the year to improve myself. Then, after I've jotted down 10 or 12 things, I date the paper and put it into the envelope and seal it.

"Next, I'll put it into a drawer and leave it there until July 1. But during those six months, my goals are working on my subconscious, and I find myself working toward them. So when I pull the envelope out on July 1, I'm often surprised at the things I can cross off. As for the ones I haven't licked, I continue to work on them. They go back into the drawer and into my subconscious again, and by the end of the year, I cross those off—if I've finished them. If I haven't done them, I put them at the top of the next year's list."

But goal setting isn't something that occurs in a vacuum. There are other influences, particularly those in our personal lives and family relationships, that may make the formulation of personal and career goals easier or harder. We've found that clear goals and supportive parents are two factors that may be closely connected in the formula for success.

Specifically, 28 percent of our respondents said their parents influenced their life goals a great deal. An additional 41 percent answered that their parents were somewhat important in helping them formulate goals. The other most frequently mentioned positive source of goal setting for high achievers was a schoolteacher or professor.

One university professor told us that the keys to his success have been well-defined goals and wonderful parents. He also reports a happy childhood, strong support from his parents, and a strong religious upbringing. But he doesn't believe in a supreme being.

He is, in fact, an avid reader, having read approximately 50 books during the past year. One interesting footnote here: He reports that the Bible is the book that had the greatest impact on his life.

Although this professor has always had very clear goals for his career, he has not had clear-cut goals for his life in general. Now in his 60s, he rates himself well above average in achieving career goals. And he is in the process of setting other goals, including more reading, writing, and travel than his busy work schedule now permits.

In fact, two thirds of our successful individuals report personal goals that they are *still* striving toward. For example:

- A psychiatrist in private practice would like "to participate in social movements for peace, a nuclear freeze," and other such causes.
- An attorney in his 70s who has already achieved a high degree of success in his career wants to "make better provisions for my family, make further contributions to society, and learn to face and accept death." This man's success has brought him many material benefits, such as two homes, several cars, a swimming pool, valuable antiques, a pleasure boat, modern video equipment, and original artwork. But now, he apparently plans to work more on his personal philosophy of life.

Self-Reliance Principle 2: Ability to exercise willpower

Chances are that if you asked a group of successful people to describe their greatest strengths, every second individual you talked to would include willpower in the list. And sure enough, over half of those we interviewed gave themselves an A in willpower.

Among other things, willpower encompasses the ability to be a self-starter and to persevere after a project has begun. Art Linkletter has long been an advocate of a particular type of willpower, which he describes by what he calls the "rule of 10." In his *Yes, You Can,* he puts it this way: "If anything is worth trying at all, it's worth trying at least 10 times. Then, if you're still not succeeding on the 11th try, reevaluate your techniques or drop the project altogether."

In short, grit your teeth and keep at a project until you've exhausted every reasonable possibility. If, after all this effort and determination, you can't make a go of it, don't beat a dead horse! Move on to the next project!

A certified public accountant who developed his company into one of the largest accounting firms in his Northwestern community told us, "The formula for success in my field is not only pride in what I do but also the guts and stamina to work the hours required to accomplish the objectives."

Now in his 60s and very happy with his family and personal life, this accountant rates himself high in willpower, hard work, an ability to get things done, and self-reliance.

Also, in his case, the willpower is rooted in a spiritual foundation. This successful businessperson believes strongly that he has a personal relationship with God and that God has a plan for his life. In fact, the Bible is the book he names as having the greatest impact on his life.

He still manages to garden and golf and to maintain an active schedule of community service. His goals for the future? "I want to be effective in keeping the local business community a viable place to live and work," he told us.

And he seems well on the way to achieving this objective. Currently, he is the chairman of a local Chamber of Commerce, serves on a hospital board, and is a member of several other committees involved in civic improvement.

Another top achiever, a senior partner in a prominent law firm, cited stamina as an essential factor for his success. He also insists that we "give attention to good health and energy as essential for success. Without a strong constitution and good physiology, no one can be successful for long." He rated himself A— for willpower and A+ in diligence.

What does he see as the source of his willpower?

It's not religion, as was the case with the accountant in the previous example. This attorney indicated only a moderate level of belief in a supreme being, with a rating of 5 out of a possible 10; and as for any personal relationship he has with God, he gave that only a 3.

Apparently, he believes that willpower has to begin with human grit and determination and be supported by physical ability to carry the load. And his life offers living support for his convictions: He's still very active in his law practice, despite the fact that he's in his 70s.

So even though these men acknowledge quite different sources for their innate willpower, both agree it's a vital link for achievement. In their minds, it takes a sound blend of mental and physical determination to lead to a successful endeavor.

To summarize: Self-reliant people will typically be able to rely on themselves to set well-defined goals and to apply willpower to persevere and realize those goals. Above all, they will fall back on their powers and resources, perhaps with some affirmation of Emerson's conviction, "Nothing at last is sacred but the integrity of your own mind."

SUCCESS CHARACTERISTIC 4: General Intelligence

General intelligence is essential for any outstanding achievement in every field because it involves your natural ability to comprehend difficult concepts quickly and to analyze them clearly and incisively. That may be an overly simplistic statement; it may even be somewhat elitist. But it does seem to represent what we found in our studies of the nation's most successful people.

But what exactly is general intelligence?

Recent studies suggest that many types of intelligence can't be measured in usual ways, such as by an IQ test. These include a *creative* intelligence, which may characterize great writers and artists; a *physical* intelligence, which can be found in great dancers and athletes; and so on.

Still, it's interesting that the successful people we interviewed—from corporate executive, to writer, to artist, to professor—had exceptionally high IQs (the median IQ on our survey of successful people was 140).

But IQ is only one measure of the kind of innate intelligence that our respondents displayed. We found that their general intelligence, perhaps partly inherited and partly acquired, consisted of at least four elements:

- An extremely high IQ score.
- An extensive vocabulary.
- Good reading skills.
- Good writing skills.

Now, let's see what some of the successful people in our survey had to say about these and other qualities related to native intelligence.

"One's maximum state of success depends upon one's inherent intelligence," said one engineer.

And 75 percent of these successful individuals seem to fit in with this statement—they rated themselves at the top of the scale of overall intelligence with a score in the A range. Also, nearly 9 out of 10 gave their intelligence a rating of at least 7 on a scale of zero to 10 as an important contributing factor to their own success.

The engineer we mentioned earlier evaluated his intellectual capacity. "I suspect I am close to my maximum," he mused. "As an experimentalist, accumulated knowledge is very important. But I did not know this as a younger person. I regret now that sometimes I thought, 'I will not use that later in life so I will not learn it now.' Studying Latin in high school is a good example."

In the laboratory setting where he works, this engineer says he is aware of two distinctly different attitudes concerning knowledge and learning. "Two kinds of people are evident in the technical community. Some hoard ideas so that the source is evident and they gain the credit for each of their own. Others are very free in their interaction and their expressions of new ideas. It is these people who feel that a 'multiplier effect' exists for new ideas. So they are less apt to consider the number of ideas to be limited."

As for his own preference between these two types of people, he declared: "I enjoy interacting with the latter group [those who share ideas] because I find it rewarding to exchange ideas and provide learning for others as well."

In his mid-40s, this engineer rated himself an A— for general intelligence and scored himself high in related skills of reading and writing. Still, in general, he rates himself above average when evaluating his success in this field.

This engineer's income is in the high five-figure range, and he reports moderate satisfaction with his current standard of living. He also contributes money on a regular basis to the disadvantaged, to charitable causes, and to a religious organization. His religious values include a strong belief in a supreme being, but only an average rating for a personal relationship with God.

Finally, his positive feelings about the value of intelligence and intellect surface again with his advice to young people entering his field: "Understand what is the state of knowledge—then exceed it."

Another high achiever, a corporate executive in finance and economics, also considers intellectual capacity an important characteristic for success: "An inquiring mind and a broad-ranging set of interests are fundamental," he said.

This executive has a lot of company. A high-powered intellect and a wide variety of interests were present in a number of our top achievers. In fact, one third reported that a wide variety of interests was a personal characteristic that contributed significantly to their success.

In addition to rating themselves high on general intelligence, the super successes in our survey gave themselves high marks for reading and writing skills. Nearly two thirds of the respondents gave themselves marks in the A range for both of these abilities, which many educators believe are closely tied to innate intelligence.

And there is plenty of evidence to support their high opinion of themselves in these areas. The average number of books each read during the year preceding the survey was 19, including 10 nonfiction works. Also, their writing skills apparently come in handy beyond the demands of normal writing for work and business correspondence. Seventy-two percent have written a letter to a political official or signed a political petition within the past year.

A way with words—and especially a broad vocabulary— has always been regarded as an important attribute for an above-average level of achievement, even for people whose main work doesn't involve high-level professional writing.

In 1983 the Johnson O'Connor Research Foundation conducted a scientific study of vocabulary levels among corporate executives. This project involved 5,000 men and women, each a president of a large U.S. company. The results? The company presidents as a whole had a higher average "Vocabulary Scale Score" than did a control group of average test takers. Also, of those presidents who participated, half scored at or above the 75th percentile for an average group of test takers.

Of course, the debate over the accuracy of IQ scores or

of any overall standard to measure general intelligence is still raging in scientific and educational circles. We can only report the facts we get and then let the chips fall where they may.

Clearly, many of the people we interviewed felt that their high intelligence had been a major factor in their success. It wasn't just common sense; it wasn't just hard work; it wasn't just a desire to excel; and it wasn't just concern for other people—though all those factors were important. These top achievers see raw brain power as a big ingredient in their personal success formulas. But they're not just talking about intelligence for its own sake. Rather, it's what that intelligence can do when it's mixed with many other key ingredients into the brew of success.

One economics expert who rated himself at the A+ level for general intelligence summed up the significance of brain power quite well when he said, "In the long run, there just is no substitute for competence." And that brings us naturally to our next major success characteristic, the ability to get things done.

SUCCESS CHARACTERISTIC 5: The Ability to Get Things Done

A finance executive told us that success depends on "an ability to organize one's time, to clearly establish one's goals, and then to pursue them with a minimum of distraction and wasted effort. In short, it is important to distinguish between what is important and what is not important."

Nearly three fourths of our high achievers ranked themselves very efficient in their ability to get things done. But how do they do it with so many conflicting demands?

They agree that at least three important qualities have

helped them produce prodigious amounts of high-quality work. These are:

- Good organizational ability.
- Productive work habits.
- Hard work and diligence.

Of course, these qualities are intimately interconnected. It's hard to be organized without good work habits, and good work habits always include hard work and diligence.

Yet, some people who have a great deal of native ability have problems getting their act together so that they can finish projects faster and more efficiently than their peers. In fact, some people who seem likely to succeed actually run an extremely high risk of *not* succeeding. These are compulsive perfectionists.

Addressing this phenomenon in *Psychology Today,* Dr. David D. Burns explains that perfectionists are not individuals who are in "healthy pursuit of excellence." Rather, "perfectionists are people who strain compulsively toward impossible goals and measure their self-worth entirely in terms of their achievements. As a result, they are terrified by the prospect of failure. They feel driven and, at the same time, unrewarded by their accomplishments."[1]

In fact, Burns goes so far as to suggest that perfectionists might succeed "in spite of their high standards, not *because* of them." It seems, in other words, that the perfection trap is extremely deadly in terms of productivity because everything becomes an all-or-nothing proposition.

Burns has one good recommendation for overcoming this

---

[1] Quoted in *Reader's Digest,* March 1985, pp. 74–75.

self-defeating habit: Always aim just for a good performance—not a masterpiece.

Once you've gotten rid of any perfectionist tendency, however, the question still remains: What's the best way to get things done?

As we've already indicated, our study suggests that the best method for getting things done is to rely on plain, old-fashioned hard work, channeled through good planning and organization and applied consistently over long periods of time.

A physics professor summarizes this particular success formula like this: "Sheer hard, tenacious work with the ability to pace oneself."

He admits working between 96 to 100 hours a week because he's dedicated to his profession. Yet, he's also quick to point out that he gives high priority to his family relationships and special cultural interests.

In fact, this professor's role models were also hard-working, highly successful individuals in their respective fields. He names Albert Einstein, Albert Schweitzer, and Frédéric Francois Chopin as some of those who significantly influenced his early life.

He also believes in getting things done outside the workplace. With an annual income in the high five figures, he has channeled his material goods into causes he supports, especially the arts and those people who are in some way less fortunate than himself.

His motives for this philanthropy seem to come from his religious values: He rates his personal relationship with God as a 10. Also, he considers himself committed to the pursuit of "ideals, integrity, and refinement."

In his self-analysis, this professor sees himself as very organized with good work habits and very high general intelligence. But, ironically, he still only rates himself a modest B+ for getting things done.

SUCCESS CHARACTERISTIC 6: Leadership

Leadership is one of the higher rated personal characteristics for those who have attained success, with 67 percent of our high achievers giving themselves an A.

But the kind of leadership they mean is not the type that one army drill sergeant used when he said, after a recruit reached his 200th push-up, "Some leaders are born. I prefer to make mine."

On the contrary, the kind of leadership that the most successful people exercise is rooted in motivation, not intimidation. In fact, the ability to motivate subordinates was a recurring trait in our high achievers, with more than half giving themselves an A in the leadership category.

Where did they learn about leadership? It may be that they received first-hand instruction from following and observing those who had done a good job of leading them. More than 6 in 10 of our successful people gave themselves a rating of A for having the ability to put orders from their superiors into effect.

For many of our respondents, early leadership experience began during school years. Fifty-eight percent held a position as class officer, organization officer, or sports team captain in high school, and 46 percent were officers or team captains in their college years.

One retired journalist gave himself an A+ for his leadership ability, which he employed regularly as editor-in-chief of a major news magazine. He expressed his formula for success in this manner:

"Cultivate an interest and intelligent curiosity about current events, along with the ability to sense public interest in a situation and to express one's self clearly, interestingly, with as little personal bias as is humanly possible—then convey these faculties to your subordinates."

He attributes a large part of his success to a healthy respect for his peers and his ability to motivate subordinates.

SUCCESS CHARACTERISTIC 7: Knowing Right from Wrong

Successful people tend to have a strong sense of right and wrong. In fact, two thirds of those we polled responded that they have a very strong moral and ethical sensitivity.

It's also true that only 43 percent reported a strong belief in a supreme being. And only 21 percent considered their personal relationship with God a high priority, worthy of a 9 or 10 rating on a scale of 10. But the moral values of right and wrong have apparently been instilled in our high achievers, regardless of their religious convictions.

There's of course a great deal more to say on this subject. So we'll evaluate the relationship between religion, morality, and success in more detail in a later chapter.

SUCCESS CHARACTERISTIC 8: Creativity

Nearly two thirds of those responding to our *Who's Who* survey said that creativity and inventiveness are very important personal skills they possess. But this is a slippery quality to define because creativity means something a little different to each individual and in each line of work.

Still, most people seem to feel that creativity and inventiveness arise from two key sources—(1) a person's reservoirs of natural talent and (2) that quasi-metaphysical concept we call "insight" or "intuition." So let's explore these two areas a little more closely and see what we can discover about the true nature of creativity.

A Talent Show for Top Achievers

"Talent is a cheap commodity—motivation makes it work," declared an innovative artist from the Midwest.

In fact, only 33 percent of the *Who's Who* achievers rated themselves at the very top, with a 9 or 10, for having a special talent that contributed to their success. Another 51 percent gave themselves a 6 to 8 mark.

The message seems to be that natural gifts are important; but at the same time, the commitment to make the best use of whatever native abilities you have is even more essential.

The Midwestern artist we quoted above is an architectual sculptor and portraitist in the medium of bronze, a field where talent is often thought to be the primary commodity. But interestingly, he rated his talent a relatively modest 8 as a contributing factor to his success. On the other hand, he gave an emphatic 10 to the importance of hard work. And he was by no means alone in these opinions: Two out of three of the successful people we interviewed agreed with him on this point.

In addition to plain old hard work, this seasoned professional artist also regards ambition, motivation, and a desire to excel in school as more crucial to success in art than special talent. A sage of sorts for the artistic community, he still maintains a heavy workload as he approaches his 80s. To keep his income fairly stable—a concern for any independent operator who makes a living in the arts—he works on 20 projects at all times. Yet his earnings are under $20,000 a year.

It's clear, then, that although this successful sculptor relies on his natural artistic gifts, he also has learned to rely on his ability to market those gifts.

Finally, what constitutes success for this man? It's not just his accomplishments in his field, which are considerable. Instead, he looks for the approval of those outside the arts community—specifically to his listing in *Who's Who*—as the most tangible evidence of his artistic achievement!

Intuition: An important door to creativity

An economist from the Southeast told us he believes that intuition arises naturally from great personal ability and talent. In a rather complete statement of his position on this point, he says: "I know that many people believe that motivation and persistence are more important than natural ability. But I disagree! They are to some extent interchangeable, but talent and ability lead to the insights that are basic to true creativity."

This man, active in economic research as well as teaching, sees his innate talents as having contributed significantly to his success and scores his talent a 9 as a contributing factor to his achievements. Furthermore, he believes this talent is absolutely essential to the intuitive abilities he uses on the job.

"*Intuition* is the sweetest fruit of natural ability," he contends. "A proposition is proven for the first time because we realize intuitively that it is true. We then search for a method of proof or verification." So he considers his intuitive insights to be invaluable to creativity.

As a matter of fact, 63 percent of our high achievers identified intuition as one of their most important personal characteristics, deserving of an A rating on their self-appraisals. Similarly, 63 percent of our high achievers also gave both willpower and creativity A ratings.

The above economist, by the way, gave himself a perfect A+ for self-reliance as well as for intuition, willpower, and creativity.

But he has more than just intuition and other success-related qualities working in his favor. He also has an IQ score of 180, a Ph.D., and a salary approaching the six-figure bracket. His success has rewarded him in deeper ways as well: He says his home life is extremely satisfying, and he considers himself very happy and content in general.

So it's true that this economist relies heavily on his intuition. But he sees it and uses it as part of a greater scheme of success that goes far beyond any one success characteristic.

SUCCESS CHARACTERISTIC 9: Self-Confidence

Over 6 out of 10 of the successful people we surveyed gave themselves a grade in the A range for self-confidence. But what exactly is self-confidence? And how do you get it?

We put this question to several highly successful people and received remarkably similar answers. Here is a typical response from Ron Nessen, former White House press secretary for Gerald Ford and former White House correspondent for NBC:

"I've always felt the way to build self-confidence is to make very careful preparations for any kind of encounter you're about to have," said Nessen, who is now a Washington, D.C. public relations executive. "So, if you're going to go on TV, be interviewed, or have an important meeting, you should read all the necessary background material. Also, you should familiarize yourself with other participants.

"In addition, you might think through possible scenarios about how the upcoming encounter might go and try to anticipate possible problems.

"I err on the side of overpreparation. But by doing that, I tend to feel more confident that I can handle the most difficult situations."

Nessen applied these principles regularly to the White House briefings he conducted for the press during the Ford administration. For example, the first time he met the press he was understandably nervous.

"I had always been on the other side of the podium, as a White House correspondent," he recalled. "I was asking the questions in those days. But now, all of a sudden, I was the one answering the questions."

President Ford helped a great deal at Nessen's first briefing by giving him a glowing introduction. "That helped to ease the way because he had a very relaxed way about him. And everyone perceived that I had his full support and backing," Nessen said.

But still, Nessen prepared to the last detail for this meeting as well as for the others he had while he served as press secretary. "There's a whole procedure of preparation for those White House briefings," he explained. "It's a several-hour procedure that used to take up almost my entire morning at the White House.

"I'd begin by reading the morning paper as I took the car to the office in the morning. Then, there would be a whole series of meetings with the senior White House staff. Part of that time was devoted to anticipating what would be asked at my briefing. As we talked, I'd gather the facts and information I expected would be necessary to answer the questions. Or if the answer depended on some decision being made by the president, I'd ask him about it.

"As we prepared, we would write down all the questions that we thought would be asked and then go over each answer to be sure they were right."

Preparation. In fact, overpreparation. That was the secret to Ron Nessen's self-confidence as he faced the toughest questions from the nation's top journalists. And his approach is almost the same as that of mutual fund sage John Templeton.

"Everybody feels more comfortable in making a presentation about a subject on which he's an expert," Templeton told us. "If your talent is playing a violin and you've practiced adequately, you won't feel at all uncertain about getting up

79

and performing. But in my case, I have no talent of that type whatever. It would be ridiculous for me to get up and try to play the violin—even if I practiced at it."

Nor does this litany of preparation, preparation, preparation end with these two accomplished individuals. Listen to Donald V. Seibert, former chair and CEO of J. C. Penney and now chairman of the American Retail Federation. In his book *The Ethical Executive,* he says: "I've come to the conclusion that all self-confidence . . . stems from three major sets of factors: (1) solid study and preparation, (2) persistence and practice, and (3) a *willingness* to be self-confident and not be content with failure."[2]

Self-confidence, then, is an inner feeling of assurance that arises from a knowledge that you've done all you can to prepare for some test, such as an important business encounter. But self-confidence among the most successful people is a *reasonable* quality. It doesn't prompt a person to take foolhardy risks—only those risks that hold the promise of success.

The top achievers we polled showed a definite willingness to strike out in new, uncharted directions: Nearly 6 in 10 gave themselves a high 9 or 10 rating for not being afraid to pursue new ideas and ventures or take risks. But in this case, the focus may have been more on the "new ideas" part of the questions than on the "risks." Only 32 percent were willing to give themselves a 9 or 10 in response to the statement, "I am not afraid to take chances or risks." And a few more, 4 out of 10, replied strongly that they are not afraid to be different.

So it appears that most successful people are highly confident about taking chances in some areas of their lives and

---

[2]   Donald V. Seibert and William Proctor, *The Ethical Executive* (New York: Simon & Schuster, 1984), p. 25.

careers, but not in all. They seem to have the greatest feelings of security in those areas where they have special expertise and in those where they are best prepared.

Finally, feelings of self-esteem may be the key to the self-confidence felt by many top achievers. First of all, they tend to be realistic about their talents and their abilities as well as about their weaknesses. So they are in a position to learn from their mistakes, even as they *expect* to reach their goals. In short, they're positive thinkers, par excellence—as least in those areas where they know they are able to excel.

So, when these top achievers do succeed, they generally feel good about themselves. In fact, the large majority were generally satisfied with all the major facets of their lives—their education, their spouse, their standard of living, the way they get along with their children, their family life, and their work.

SUCCESS CHARACTERISTIC 10: Oral Expression

Successful individuals need to communicate effectively—a call sounded over and over today. And true to form, the majority of our top achievers rated their oral skills at the top of the scale.

First of all, they're confident of their ability to speak in public, with 64 percent giving themselves an A grade. Also, 57 percent put themselves at the A level for their conversational ability.

Some highly successful people develop their oral skills at a relatively young age. Investor John Templeton, for example, says, "The first times I ever appeared publicly were in a high school dramatic production and also as part of a debating and declaiming society. And when I stood before an audience of 100 to 200 people, I understood the meaning of stage fright."

But instead of running away from the challenge, Templeton faced it directly. "I reasoned with myself. I said, No one expects me to be perfect. Obviously, I'm *not* perfect. All I can do is the best job I know how. If I pray ahead of time, I'm likely to do as well as God wants me to. So there's no reason to be shy or frightened about it."

Since the time he was 12 or 13, Templeton says, "I haven't felt any stage fright about making a public appearance." Today, he regularly speaks to thousands at stockholder meetings for his mutual funds and to millions in his radio and television appearances.

Donald Seibert, former CEO of J. C. Penney, had a somewhat different experience with public speaking. He says he did well speaking extemporaneously before small groups when he first started to move up in his company. But when more than 8 or 10 sat before him, he felt his stomach get tied up in knots.

Although it took about 15 years and even a couple of visits to a physician to get some tips on handling stress, he finally worked things out. He discovered that when he felt himself tightening up, he could just take a deep breath and walk to the side of the podium—and that would usually cause him to relax. Apparently, there was some sort of physiological buildup of inner tension that was released when he moved about while speaking.

But Seibert, like most other achievers, knew he had to keep working at his ability to express himself orally. His success depended upon it.

SUCCESS CHARACTERISTIC 11: Concern for Others

The old saw, "It's not what you know, but who you know" might be altered somewhat by our top achievers to read: "It's not what you know, but who you know—and how well you get along with them."

A solid two out of three rated an A in their ability to

get along with other people. But this does not reflect an attitude of "peace at any price." Only 36 percent considered themselves so tolerant of others' viewpoints that they were willing to give themselves a 9 or 10 rating. Another 39 percent gave a 9 or 10 response to the statement: "I care a great deal about other people."

On the other hand, about half—51 percent—of our high achievers said that they regarded caring about other people as an extremely important trait that had contributed to their success. Apparently, then, there's some tension between how these achievers view their own concern for others and how they think that concern has helped them in their work. It seems that they know it's important to care for others on the job; but perhaps they feel they haven't developed quite far enough in this area.

On the other hand, some successful people—at least a third of those we polled—do think they're especially strong in their concern for others.

"I care about people as a whole—not their warts," wrote one psychiatrist. "I see their potential instead of their values, which are very important as well. But without the capacity to use one's potential, what are values?"

Now in his mid-70s, this psychiatrist is still practicing on a private basis. He considers two factors as primary marks of his success: (1) that he's been responsive to his patients' needs and (2) that he's earned the respect of his colleagues. Although his earnings range between $50,000 and $100,000 annually, he indicated that he places a rather low value on material things as a reward of success.

How did he develop his deep concern for others?

He came to a kind of crossroads during his military service. "I believe my injury in World War II refocused my life. My rehabilitation changed my outlook on life and medicine and turned me toward psychiatry."

None of his humanitarian attitudes seem connected with

any religious conviction, however. He rates his belief in a supreme being at 1 on a scale of zero to 10, and he says he has no personal relationship with God. But at the same time, he is emphatic in his sense of knowing right from wrong. And he believes in applying his humanistic value system to his practice of psychiatry, his relationships with others, and his evaluation of personal success.

These remarks reflect the sentiments of those who have a deep concern for others or regard this quality as a factor contributing greatly to their own success. But what about those successful people who don't feel quite so strongly about this issue?

Most of the people we surveyed at least placed themselves and the value of caring for others in the upper-middle part of the scales we provided. But many of our respondents had only a mildly positive attitude toward this characteristic. Why?

Part of the answer could be ambition and the tension that naturally arises between competing with others and helping them out. Successful people have a strong if not overwhelming desire to succeed. Success doesn't happen to them by accident. As a result, they find they have to run the race faster than other people who work with them. If they are to win, then almost everyone else must lose.

In this regard, it's helpful to refer to Douglas LaBier, a psychoanalyst in Washington, D.C., who deals with disillusioned careerists regularly at the Project on Technology, Work, and Character. In 1983, after six years of study on emotional problems from work-related stress, LaBier concluded that "half of those considered successful by their peers are unhappy."

He believes that their ambitions lead them to "subscribe to the values of their companies in order to get ahead." And, in many cases, these company values may be incompatible with their own. In other words, ambition triumphs over all else.

Half of the individuals from our *Who's Who* study did give themselves a top rating in ambition and the desire to get ahead, although only 8 percent are highly motivated by a strong desire to make money.

But where LaBier found a high level of discontent among successful people, we found an extremely high level of general satisfaction. A solid 53 percent of our top achievers listed themselves as very happy, and 41 percent said they were fairly happy. Only 2 percent considered themselves not too happy with their lives.

SUCCESS CHARACTERISTIC 12: Luck

Writing in *Redbook* magazine in May 1984, Jeffrey Blum proposed several rules for "How to Get Lucky." These included:

- Work hard to get lucky.
- Figure out the source of your failure and pain— then change it.
- Avoid negative thought patterns and create positive, optimistic ones.
- Take reasonable risks and experiment with new opportunities.
- Don't push your luck.
- Do unto others as you would have them do unto you.

But that's just the beginning of what our top achievers had to say about luck in their lives. So we've decided to devote the entire next chapter to the fascinating topic of the role that good fortune plays in success.

CHAPTER

THE RIGHT PLACE AT THE RIGHT TIME

Question: What do you regard as the key factors that contributed to your success in your field?
Answer: Luck—being born on the right planet, in the right epoch.

Carl Sagan, scientist and "planetary explorer"

Luck.

Some people say you make your own. Others claim you have no control over it. Still others believe that some divine providence is orchestrating all the coincidences, accidents, and strokes of fate that punctuate our lives.

But whatever the explanation, there's no doubt about one thing: The "slings and arrows of outrageous fortune," as Shakespeare put it in "Hamlet," are an ever-present factor in success and achievement in our lives.

One administrator of a large state agency framed the issue best:

"I have long felt that timing and good fortune—serendipity, if you will—play a significant role in success, assuming that the individual is otherwise capable. Life is an endless series of forks in the road requiring constant decisions and choices. I can think of many occasions when an alternative choice of my own would have led, I think, to greater success of one kind or another."

Luck, indeed, almost always plays some sort of role in any individual's success. Several decades ago, a highly confident young actor once wrote in his diary: "I have a fierce energy and passion and a thinking brain and a powerful emotion. No one can take those things from me."

He was equally sure his talent would break through for all to see. "The directors here will find out. . . ." he declared at one point.

But the directors didn't find out. The time, the place, and the person weren't quite right.

On the contrary, the young actor, whose name was Clifford Odets, turned out to be a failure as a stage performer. Unrealistic and stilted, he simply wasn't sufficiently talented to compete with his fellow actors. Predictably, the directors he had counted on to recognize his talent cast him in insignificant parts.

Still, he persevered, happy even to have bit parts in the productions being done by the Group Theatre, an experimental acting and production company in New York. But things never worked out. So Odets began to shift his aspirations and energies in a different direction. He decided to focus on writing plays.

But Odets didn't start off with a bang in this field either. He took two acts of a play he had written to director Harold Clurman but found little encouragement. Neither Clurman nor the legendary acting guru Lee Strasberg believed that the young actor had any talent as a playwright.

It looked as if Odets had failed at *two* vocations in the theater. But the aspiring playwright wasn't about to quit—in part because of commitment to the field of the theater and in part because of necessity. In short, he had no other way to make a living.

So he stayed with the Group Theatre as an actor and continued to write. It was a hard grind, trying to pursue two full-time career goals at the same time. And failure seemed to stalk him wherever he turned. He worked as an understudy, not even landing bit parts that he could perform regularly before live audiences. Simultaneously, he kept churning out pages for a new play. This one, entitled "Victory," was received even less enthusiastically than the partial script he had offered earlier to Clurman.

But Odets refused to throw in the towel. The would-be actor and playwright continued to play small parts whenever he could get hired and kept scribbling away at his next play, which finally became his ticket to the big time. This work, "Awake and Sing," surprised many people by becoming a Broadway sensation. His next work was "Waiting for Lefty," followed closely by "Golden Boy," a major hit of the period. "Golden Boy" later became a popular musical with Sammy Davis, Jr., in the lead role.

Clifford Odets had finally found success.

But consider his career pattern, if you can call it that. He certainly never became the great actor he wanted to be. In fact, he really didn't know where he was going until after he got there.

But he did try several approaches to success in the theater, and he refused to accept defeat. And just as important, he waited until his time had finally arrived. In short, he eventually found himself in the right place at the right time. You might say he was lucky. But he made his own luck by working hard, attacking his chosen field from several directions, and being patient.[1]

---

[1]   For a complete treatment of Odets's life and work, see Margaret Brenman-Gibson, *Clifford Odets: American Playwright—the Years From 1906 to 1940* (New York: Atheneum Publishers, 1982).

Odets isn't alone in his experience with finding success. Another Depression-era writer, Raymond Chandler, directed independent oil companies before he started a career writing detective stories at age 45. Artists Paul Gauguin and Henri Rousseau spent years as a stockbroker and a customs collector, respectively, before they produced the paintings that established their place in history.

This is not a plug for changing careers in midlife. Rather, the background of these American and European success stories demonstrates that not everyone plans where they are going before starting a career. In fact, many who *do* plan end up somewhere else anyway. The factors of chance and timing always have to be included in any equation for success.

If you've ever surprised yourself by impulsively taking advantage of a sudden opportunity—in effect, leaping off a cliff to follow a wild, unproven idea—you aren't alone. The guts to pursue new ideas and ventures—to be willing to take risks— looms large in the minds of many successful people. In fact, nearly 6 in 10 of the top achievers we surveyed rated this trait as extremely important for their own success. Furthermore, 38 percent ranked pure luck as a major success-producing factor in their career experience, and 31 percent gave the highest marks to choosing the right field at the right time.

But, as we'll see, mere luck, accidental timing, and risk taking aren't all there is to it. Although many successful people seem to be putting on a high wire act that remains beyond the capability of the rest of us, behind the dramatic posturing often lies years of hard work. Then, opportunity knocks. And the background of preparation provides a platform to leap out and grasp any lucky circumstances that may beckon.

To see how luck and fortuitous timing have operated in the lives of some other successful people, consider a few additional examples. One music critic we interviewed was particularly straightforward about the luck issue: "If there is any formula (which I doubt, regardless of the field involved) it is the luck of having the right interests at the right time."

In his case, he started writing about recorded music well before the field of music criticism began to expand "from a few fanatics in a hobby/cult, to an eventually mass-public interest." He also says that a classic book he wrote on music "came out at just the right time to win worldwide attention."

Yet, in his youth, this man displayed certain traits that helped him take full advantage of his later luck. He always liked reading, writing, and music. He also wrote for and edited his high school magazine.

In addition, he knew what his priorities in life should be—even when those priorities prompted him to break rules. For example, he says he "always played hooky Fridays to go into Boston . . . to join the Boston Symphony Concerts rush line (then only 25 cents for any seat in the second balcony)!"

The risk-taking didn't end with these childhood exploits. Although he had a full-tuition scholarship to Harvard, he decided the Ivy League was not for him and quit after a couple of months. Instead, he enrolled in a leading music conservatory.

Despite his auspicious academic potential, this man feels that his formal education failed to prepare him either for his later work as a music critic or for life in general. Instead, his primary education seems to have come from the books he read and from his own practical experience.

In fact, this writer still reads prodigiously, revealing that, until lately, he's read well over 400 books a year! Now, he's dropped to a mere 200 per annum! And they are heavy tomes: philosophy, history, and musical theory.

In short, this music writer has made his own mold for success. He followed his inner lights, worked hard to do what he liked best, and consistently happened to be in the right place at the right time.

But it's important for us not to end with a simplistic sum-up here. Luck and timing were extremely important for this man, but at the same time, he had to be ready to seize and make the most of the opportunities that came his way.

A top achiever in an entirely different field saw the relationship between luck and preparation in much the same way. As the CEO of a large insurance company with an annual income well in excess of $200,000 a year, this man summarized his formula for success this way: "(1) reasonable level of intelligence; (2) hard work coupled with long hours; and (3) a good education."

But then he added a key fourth factor: "Luck."

He explained, "Given basic good education and good health, it seems to me that individual drive, initiative, and efficient hard work are the ingredients of success—provided the person has a well-balanced personality and high ethical standards. These attributes will position you to exploit good luck and contain the effects of bad luck."

Another who has always been quick to seize opportunities is an artist, now in his mid-30s. He lives on the West Coast and earns an annual income in the $20,000 to $50,000 range.

In words that echo the personal success philosophy of others we've studied, he said, "Success is achieved when opportunity meets preparedness. However, you must recognize the opportunity and not be afraid to act and take a chance."

In other parts of the survey, he indicated that he considers luck, timing, and being at the right place at the right time as ranking among the most important factors in his success.

But there's considerably more to this man's success than just taking advantage of opportunities. He's also an independent thinker who isn't willing to make a commitment to just anything that comes along. On the contrary, he also has to be deeply interested in the opportunities that present themselves.

"Jobs should be chosen from personal desire," he declared. "You cannot excel or be happy unless you love what you do."

So liking your work is just the first step. To rise toward peaks of accomplishment, however, it's necessary to do much more. Some of the extra requirements that have catapulted this artist to success come through in the advice he gives to those just entering his field:

- Work to develop the craft.
- Believe you're good.
- Work hard all the time.
- Take advantage of opportunities.

Work . . . believe . . . work . . . take advantage. It's all there, so simple to say and understand and yet so hard to make the commitment required for great achievement.

One other thing that comes across clearly in this artist's responses is that he's enthusiastic about nearly everything and overwhelmingly positive. He's also incredibly organized, dedicated, and disciplined. He puts a high priority on establishing goals, ambition, and maintaining good work habits.

Obviously, with this artist and with others in artistic fields, passion and raw talent don't do the trick alone. There must be a personal backup system, such as goal setting and good work habits. These are substantially the same backup systems and attitudes that result in success for anyone—business leader, professor, research scientist, or painter.

So it's certainly significant that this man says he's not afraid to be different, not afraid to take chances or risks, and not afraid to pursue new ideas or ventures. But it's also significant that he plans ahead for these venturesome enterprises.

Luck for this man, then, is largely luck that he made himself. He began his fast track to success with a good academic record—top quarter of his high school class, honors graduate from college, and a masters degree. So with this native intellectual ability and his practical work ability, it's understandable and believable when he says he would have been successful in a field other than art.

We expect him to succeed in whatever he attempts because we know he'd only go into a line of work that he could get passionate about and one that he would feel he had the talent to pursue. And we also know that, once he got into that other field, he would bring his work habits and other success-producing traits to bear.

This takes us back to how schooling influences success. An artist may not be what we would normally regard as a businessperson. But without many of the same skills and characteristics that lead to success in business, the efforts of any artist will almost surely come to nothing.

Opportunity or good fortune usually knocks at some point for most people. But if it knocks before they develop many of the key personal characteristics associated with success, they may not be in a position to grab the opportunity and run with it. You won't be able to take an *appropriate risk*—or be able to leap off the cliff and be fairly certain to land safely.

But, having said all this, we still must recognize the serendipitous quality that ultimately characterizes all luck. The bottom line is that sometimes you just can't exercise control over the most magnificent kind of luck. You simply have to let it happen.

What we're referring to here is that once-in-a-lifetime surprise that strikes only a few of the most accomplished individuals in our society. It may be the Nobel prize, the position of chief executive officer, or the bestseller that stays at the top of a national list for two years.

Many in a given field work hard, and a number become successful by most definitions. But there may be only one person who really hits the top.

That's what happened to one microbiologist who spent years of his life single-mindedly working toward his goal of becoming a doctor. He never had an outside job while he was in school, and he worked hard, with consistently well-defined goals both in school and in his chosen field.

Like many of our other successes, he always read much more than others his age, and he graduated in the top 10 percent of his class, both in high school and college. As he was growing up, this future doctor got along well with his parents and was fairly happy. But his life seemed to be mostly a single-minded, hard-working, focused effort in one direction.

And it paid off. His scientific discovery resulted in the creation of a multimillion-dollar industry. What pushed him to the top of his field? He lists the factors this way:

"1. To be in the field of biology and medical laboratory work.
2. To be a medical doctor.
3. Strong motivation, specialized knowledge, hard work, common sense, puzzle-solving activity in my laboratory work.
4. To be at the right place at the right time and to have the perception or intuition of scientific novelty."

He further emphasizes this luck factor elsewhere in the survey as a key component in the greatest event of his life, his major scientific discovery. For example, when asked what experiences in his chosen field have contributed most to his success, he gives exceptionally high ratings to luck and choosing the right field at the right time.

In this doctor's case, then, it's certainly important to credit the hard work and preparation that went before. But it's also essential to understand that an unpredictable element of chance may enter in to carry an individual to the peak of achievement.

In fact, sometimes a person gets on such a fast track to success that taking chances, seizing opportunities, and juggling the vagaries of luck become a way of life. A book publisher we encountered is somewhat like this. He's living his career like an Olympian going for a gold medal. At only 41, he already feels that he's made a difference in the world by the way he's done his work. He says he's published books no one else would have published—books of lasting cultural value.

Like many of our other risk takers, he's not afraid to be different. And he combines a special talent in a specific area with something he values even more—common sense.

One of the ways he uses his common sense is to plan. His plan for young people who want to enter his field is to: (1) read widely, (2) determine what you like to read, and find out who published it, and (3) campaign to work for that publisher. This advice is simple and straightforward.

This publisher also has a plan for what he's going to do next in his life. But that isn't the key for him. He'd rather take what comes and improvise with it, follow the leads, whatever they are.

"Success really depends on one's ability or willingness to accept circumstance and opportunity and make the best of them," he says. "One should do one's best in all things and follow one's strengths and strongest interests. There can be no grand plan that works: all is creative extemporization."

But sometimes a heavy emphasis on good fortune, with a lack of any sense of a grand plan, may result in feelings of uncertainty, confusion, and even chaos—even in the midst of great individual achievement.

For example, one social science professor punctuated his entire questionnaire with references to what he perceived as the incredible role of luck in his life:

- In describing his personal formula for success in his field, he replied, "Luck and work—in that order."
- When asked to rank those experiences in his field that had contributed to his success, he first listed luck, timing, and being at the right place at the right time followed by choosing the right field at the right time.

- He also gave a top score of 10 to the personal characteristic: "I was just born lucky."

But the experience of luck in this man's case left him with a rather mixed set of feelings.

"Looking back," he writes, "I would say that all matters of life and success are quite chaotic and confusing. Luck matters more than anything. I suspect that a close analysis of my answers here would reveal much that is contradictory and ambiguous. There have been few clear patterns in my life, and one is left with a general feeling of sadness about it all."

It's true that he lists himself as very happy with his life and quite satisfied with his family relationships, work, and other such things. But for all his day-to-day happiness, he still seems sad about the overview of his life. Things just don't quite fit together in a meaningful way.

So luck, by itself, won't necessarily lead to meaning and direction for a successful person. For a more comprehensive sense of purpose, it's necessary to look beyond happenstance and accident. And that need has caused some of our successful people to explore religious faith and values.

CHAPTER

RELIGION AND THE RISE TO THE TOP

Integrity . . . honesty . . . commitment to excellence which generates enthusiasm to sustain personal drive and releases powers of persuasion which attracts great support from great people who encourage unflinching determination to keep on keeping on.

Dr. Robert Schuller, founding pastor of the Crystal Cathedral

"I can't lose an election," U.S. Senator Mark Hatfield said. "My opponent may get more votes, but I still win because my commitment is to God's will.

"It's obvious to me that if an opponent gets more votes, God has some other place for me," he continued. "Therefore, I'm still the winner in seeking God's will. That's the only belief that keeps me from climbing the walls in this jungle: I don't have to worry about the next election."

A solid, outspoken minority of one in five of the successful people we polled would respond with a hearty "Amen" to Hatfield's sentiments. On a scale of zero to 10, they gave a top rating of 9 or 10 to the belief that they have a close relationship with God and that God has a plan for their lives.

Feelings run high on this issue, however. An even larger number, about two out of five, told us that they do *not* feel a close relationship with God or believe He has a plan for their lives. These people gave a zero or 1 rating to the two questions.

One of those in the nonbelieving category is a prominent sculptor who makes close to $100,000 a year and seems to have redirected any religious inclinations into his work.

"Most artists I have known see their work as a commitment, rather like a religious order," he said. "This is how they structure their lives, rather than as a career in the usual sense. Materialism as such usually involves tools or travel."

His antireligious sentiments came out strongly when we asked what books have had the greatest impact on his life. His sole response: "Not the Bible." Also, he gave decisive zero ratings to questions about whether he believes God has a plan for his life or whether he has a close personal relationship with God.

Others were more equivocal when it came to describing their religious beliefs. One poet, who styled himself as an anarchist, said, "My religious beliefs burn and fade, so those questions are impossible." And there were also a number of searchers. A literature professor told us that one of his goals for the future was "to develop a more satisfactory philosophy of life."

The questions that provoked the most negative or uncertain answers from many of our top achievers related to the degree of intimacy involved in their personal relationships with God. On the other hand, when the questions become a little less personal, the numbers begin to shift: Two out of five said they believe strongly (with a 9 or 10 rating) that a supreme being exists.

Even the sculptor we mentioned above—the one who awarded zeros to questions about his personal involvement with God—gave a rather high rating of 8 to the strength of his belief in a supreme being. In fact, only about one in five of our respondents are, in effect, outright nonbelievers or skeptics who responded with a militantly negative zero or 1 to the statement, "I believe in a supreme being."

As far as moral values in general are concerned, 67 percent responded with a 9 or 10 that they have a very strong sense of right and wrong. In fact, only 8 percent responded with a mostly negative rating of 5 or less to the statement, "I have a strong sense of right and wrong."

Figure 6-1
RELIGIOUS PREFERENCE

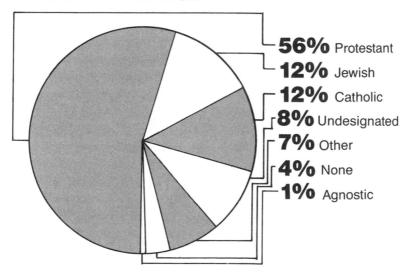

56% Protestant
12% Jewish
12% Catholic
8% Undesignated
7% Other
4% None
1% Agnostic

It seems that the idea of God and a strong sense of moral values are at least important background factors for our successful people. And for a zealous minority of about 20 percent, the personal experience of a close, caring deity has been a key ingredient in their personal and career development.

Of course, there's nothing new about connecting God with success. There are a number of examples of this in the Hebrew Scriptures, as when the Lord said to Joshua:

> "This book of the law shall not depart from your mouth, but you shall meditate on it day and night, so that you may be careful to do according to all that is written in it; for then you will make your way prosperous, and *then you will have success*" (Joshua 1:8; NAB)

With the Torah in one hand and a sword in the other, Joshua led the children of Israel into the promised land. No doubt there were people with Joshua who thought it luck or coincidence that the walls of Jericho fell just when the priests blew their shofars. But after the people had marched around the walls of the city for three days and Joshua did everything that God had commanded, no one could have convinced him that his success was the result of anything but God's providence.

In their responses, some of our interviewees affirmed Joshua's kind of faith, though a few also linked good luck with God's actions. For example, in stating his personal formula for success, the president of one university said: "You have to be lucky (in theological terms, you have to enjoy the Lord's blessing)."

Others were much more straightforward in attributing their success to the God of traditional religion. A businessperson from Virginia, with an income well into six figures, told us, "I have always felt the presence of Jesus Christ in my life. I owe all to Him."

But even though some of these top achievers affirm deep and very specific religious convictions, they all seem to be doers rather than passive believers. Of those in our survey, 96 percent told us that they gave money to a charitable cause in the last 12 months. Also, 68 percent have given to a religious organization; 43 percent have donated time to helping the poor, disadvantaged, or needy; and 31 percent have donated time specifically to religious work.

Some who believe deeply in a personal God and also give money and time to religious and charitable causes would agree with entertainer Pat Boone that the way to success, including material riches, is to "find out God's will, and then pray it into action."

As authority for this idea, Boone cites various passages of scripture, including Psalm 112: "Blessed is the man who fears the Lord. . . . Wealth and riches are in his house."

Boone also believes there's a tremendous potential to achieve success in the principle that Jesus stated in Luke 6:38: "Give, and it shall be given to you. . . . For whatever measure you deal out to others, it will be dealt to you in return." (Luke 6:38; NAB)

To illustrate this point, Boone likes to tell a personal story about how he emerged from a series of financial crises by relying on Luke 6. He was facing the loss of millions through some unfortunate business dealings, and he couldn't figure out how to resolve the problem—at least not until he turned on the radio in the car one day. A preacher came on the air and started drawing connections between giving to God's work and receiving material blessings. The main thrust of the message was: "God demands his tithe!"

Boone felt the words were directed to him because, even though he had a strong faith at the time, he wasn't giving away much of his money. So he resolved on the spot to increase his giving to 10 percent of his gross income.

The result? Within a year, he had paid all his outstanding expenses, reduced his debts, paid off all his taxes, and even started a pension fund.[1] Boone's interpretation: "It was because I was giving God 10 percent off the top."

Clearly, the 40 percent of our respondents who reject the idea of a personal relationship with God or a divine plan for their lives would also reject Pat Boone's interpretation. But that's not the point. The point is that a significant minority of successful people are quite open to this sort of spiritual explanation for success and spiritual blessings. In fact, as we'll see later, the spiritual dimension of their lives may be the major motivation—the deepest source of their sense of meaning and mission—that drives them to the top.

The spiritual factor in success comes to fruition well into adulthood, but it often begins early in childhood. In fact, one in five top achievers—the same number who put a major emphasis on religion—said that a religious upbringing was very important in their rise to the top.

Mutual fund sage John Templeton had this kind of experience. His mother was deeply involved in the Unity School of Christianity, a movement that stresses positive thinking to the extreme. In this view of reality, human beings and their institutions can always be changed for the better through prayer and love. Also, material success and wealth are supposed to arise automatically through personal spiritual development and social progress. Norman Vincent Peale was deeply influenced by this school of thought, and it became the basis for his many popular positive-thinking sermons and books.

Templeton, on the other hand, expressed this spiritual ori-

---

[1] For a further expansion of this account, see Pat Boone's *Pray To Win: God Wants You to Succeed* (New York: Popular Library, 1980).

entation in another way—by becoming a super success in the world of investments. But remember that, even though the culmination came in his adult career, the seeds were planted in the religious influences of childhood.

These, then, are some of the religious threads that run through a number of our success stories. But there's a great deal more to be said. To understand just how comprehensive the religious influence on success can be, let's consider seven "spiritual principles" that have emerged in this survey of top achievers.

SPIRITUAL PRINCIPLE 1: Be Open to a "Damascus Road Experience" in Your Career Development

The apostle Paul saw a blinding light and was instantly converted when he was heading toward Damascus to persecute the early Christians; his spiritual encounter established the standard for the dramatic conversion experience. Usually, this sort of religious watershed focuses on an overall change in the direction of one's life. But sometimes, the change may focus on one particular phase of life, such as the career.

Such was the case with a physician and faculty member at a medical school who told us, "Some uncanny events have shaped my career:

"(1) My decision to go into medicine occurred after my freshman college year in a sudden spiritual revelation that I shall never forget.

"(2) In the rare times of great personal stress (as when I lost my first wife by a chronic degenerative brain disease after 32 years of idyllic marriage), just the right person entered my life to rescue me.

"(3) Several chance occurrences have shaped my research direction in the past three years, resulting in profound change in my objectives and much closer attainment of the goal I have been seeking for 25 years.

"These experiences, among many others that have affected my family and my patients, have made me a more religious person than I ever was. I feel as though I'm a part of a very large universe that I marvel at but do not understand."

Highly intelligent, with the top grade average award in his senior year of college, this man might seem the sort who would give primary importance to brainpower in achieving success in his field. Instead, he listed these qualities as the key to top performance:

1. Humility.
2. Persistent endeavor.
3. Liking people in general.
4. Intelligent interest in the technical aspects.
5. Helping other people.

Also, he put the trait of caring about other people as his strongest personal characteristic.

Throughout his questionnaire, this doctor stressed the importance of home life during his childhood and how it had undergirded his adult achievements. He told us that he had a very happy childhood and a good relationship with his mother and father.

The youngest of two children, he said that "growing up in a top-notch academic environment in which my father was a respected professor and teacher" had a great influence on him and his goals in life. His strong religious upbringing was also an important factor that he believed contributed to his later success.

Finally, he's very happy with his life today. In our scale of 1 to 10 he gave a 10 rating to his relationship with his spouse and children, his family life in general, and his personal life. The only thing that he is *not* happy with is the way things are going in this country at this time.

Throughout his survey, this doctor indicated his belief in

an unseen but powerful divine hand that orchestrated uncanny events or revelations resulting in his present success
and happiness. In a way, his last words said it all: "I cannot
tell how much of my success I am entirely responsible for!"

SPIRITUAL PRINCIPLE 2: Put Belief above Ambition

A college coach and teacher gave us this formula for his
success:

> "1. Have integrity and sincerity, i.e., you must *be-
> lieve* and be committed to what you teach
> and do.
> "2. The first 10 years you must work very hard—
> much overtime and efficiency.
> "3. You must learn to accept your imperfections
> and curtail your ambition but *not* your deter-
> mination."

This successful hockey coach makes less than $20,000 per
year, and money has had little influence on his drive for success. He told us that for him the evidence of success was "great
enjoyment of the work, good evaluations by students, and
wide invitations to teach and preach."

Again and again in our interview, this man downplayed
ambition, the drive to get ahead, the desire for money, and
promotion of his own interests at the expense of others. *Hard
work* and *diligence* were words that constantly cropped up
in his responses.

Crucial for him was a strong religious faith, which his parents had instilled in him. Predictably, the most important
books in his life were the Bible and the writings of Augustine
and Luther.

In advising young people entering his field, he said, "In

general, be sure of and committed to your faith, though the details of your belief system can and should be doubted. Also, try several approaches to your vocation to help you find the right one; and work like hell for the first 10 years."

There are three career fields he would recommend to young people today: the ministry and teaching, public service in any of its many forms, and politics and foreign service.

And he added this: "Note: These three vocations are the hardest, least likely to succeed in, and most needed."

In closing, he offered this final observation: "A word about ambition: I had no desire to compete and beat out other people. But I was determined to do the best I could to do the job right. I had to occasionally compromise with the system, e.g., publish or perish. But even there I really wanted to write books and articles as a way of furthering the work at hand. So in summary, ambition: no; determination: yes."

SPIRITUAL PRINCIPLE 3: Nurture Your Faith Every Day

The kind of faith that seems to make a difference in achieving success is one that gives the individual inner strength on a *consistent* basis. That means nurturing the belief system regularly—usually on a daily basis—through prayer and other spiritual exercises.

A semiretired physician from Kentucky told us how he was able to overcome adverse conditions in his childhood and obtain success by experiencing this regular spiritual nurture from early childhood: "I was raised by my grandparents and a maiden aunt and, during my summer vacations, by my maternal grandmother and two aunts. My maiden aunt used to tell me tales of my future as a physician."

In fact, he said, "I knew by the time I was seven I was a physician."

Even though he was shuffled about by family members

who had very little money to support him, he said, "I have so much to be thankful for. My uncle took over my education when I was nine, and a pastor guided me through the first two years of college. I feel that I have been blessed by having been at the right place at the right time. I have been successful from the beginning. I have been able to set and to achieve my goals as I have set achievable goals and gone after them one at a time. All the way to this day *I have put my life in the hands of Divine Guidance* and have kept alive a sense of mission—that of a physician."

The people who have influenced him most in life were his uncle and his pastor. And the books that had the greatest impact were the Bible and John Bunyan's *Pilgrim's Progress.*

Although this doctor struggled up from a poor childhood during the Depression to an income of six figures, his troubles weren't over even after he reached adulthood. He told us that one great evidence of his success involved the strength of character he developed to get through some periods of bad health.

Specifically, this doctor says he's a success because he's "been able to survive chronic illness, three coronaries, a terrible bypass and to live a life of public service, to relieve pain, to interdict suffering, to promote healing of illness, and to enjoy my students and family."

A close personal relationship with God and a belief that God has a plan for his life have been constant sources of inspiration. And his formula for success has been "enjoying my work, dedication to and compassion for my patients, and treating them truly like people."

As a result of the daily relationship he has cultivated with his God, he says with the ring of assurance: "I knew without a doubt I was in my correct and predestined field of work, and I've relied completely on Divine Guidance in my day-to-day activity. All I ever dreamed of has come to me. My work has been easy."

SPIRITUAL PRINCIPLE 4: Individual Success Can Emerge Even in the Midst of Deep Dissatisfaction with Society

Social criticism and reform have been a mainstay of profound religious experience in the United States. And some of the most devastating criticism has come from some of our most religious *and* successful respondents. Try this, for example:

"What is happening to this great country is a tragedy:

- Inflation—still roaring despite what the politicians, bankers, and media say.
- Secular Humanism.
- Dope.
- Hedonism.
- Less than half the people supporting more than half.
- Jackson pitting blacks against whites.
- General selfishness, much crookedness, and an 'I'll-get-mine' attitude.
- Poor performance of Congress and the bankers. They've broken the country."

A very bleak picture indeed. Yet this comes to us from the chairman of the board and president of two debt-free, expanding manufacturing concerns. He earns an income well into six figures and possesses all the outward trappings of the most successful business leaders in the country. Yet he's convinced that the world is falling apart around him.

How does this businessperson maintain his incredible career drive in the face of his pessimism about the nation's future? In his own words: "I am a manufacturer—a creator of wealth. I took over the management of a failing company in 1948. It has grown to a fine company, 45 times its original size. I started a separate manufacturing firm from zero in

1954. It is now a good-sized firm, number one in its industry. Neither company *has a dollar of debt.*"

Despite his extensive criticisms of current cultural developments, this conservative Republican wasn't completely negative about the present American scene. In fact, he expressed a firm belief in the American system for allowing people to make their own way.

But in his opinion the system is only working when people *do* make their own way. His advice as to which fields young people should enter confirms this individualistic philosophy: "You should go into any field that creates wealth, as opposed to those fields that survive on other people's wealth."

He went on to say that, to have the best chance to succeed, young people should "work hard, be of unquestioned integrity, and use the Bible as your rock foundation and guide."

His religious allegiance is quite specific. In answer to our question about which denomination he belongs to, he said, "I believe in Jesus."

Although this man gave low ratings to social status, expensive belongings, and money to buy or do anything, he has accumulated many material blessings.

His future goals? True to his hard-driving past, he will not rest on his laurels as far as his business or his religion are concerned. He says he plans "to continue the growth of the two manufacturing concerns; help my son to take over; spend more time with my wife; and try to live to the glory of the Lord."

SPIRITUAL PRINCIPLE 5: Pray to God but Row for the Shore

An old Russian proverb says, "Pray to God, but row for the shore." And that kind of activist spirituality is what characterizes many successful people who have a deep faith.

For example, Donald Seibert, former chairman and CEO of J. C. Penney, says, "When I pray, I pray on the basis that I'm willing to be the instrument God uses to answer my own prayer. Also, if I'm concerned about some problem, I should be willing to be the solution to that problem instead of just offering up some general prayer."

In a similar vein, the president of one graduate school who responded to our survey advised young people to "work hard and use your talents faithfully; don't worry about getting money, status, or power; let providence decide how high you rise."

This man gave himself low scores on his ability to make money and willingness to be different from others, but he gave the highest score on his work habits. In confirmation of his diligence, he said his goal for the future is "writing, organizing voluminous notes on selected topics into articles and books."

His longstanding concern about spiritual matters came out when we asked what books had had the greatest impact on his life. In addition to the Bible, he listed "books on sociology, psychology, and religion."

Finally, he gave himself a perfect 10 when asked the extent to which he believes (1) that there is a supreme being, (2) that he has a close relationship with God, and (3) that God has a plan for his life.

SPIRITUAL PRINCIPLE 6: Do unto Others as You Would Have Them Do unto You

The golden rule is a basic guideline of life that consistently emerges in the answers of those top achievers who said they have a strong religious faith.

For example, an Alaskan family physician told us, "Under God, a person has a responsibility to love his neighbor and be sensitive and responsive to his needs and hurts. Also, we should use and develop the gifts, mental and spiritual, that we are endowed with; and we should honor our parents and our God and respect our fellow man. Finally, we should love our country and respect those in positions of responsibility."

This doctor indicated little interest in money, power, or status as rewards of success. Instead, he said that being able to contribute to society and having a sense of personal worth and self-respect were of primary importance to him. As for those personal traits he believes have contributed to his success, he placed hard work, common sense, and caring about other people at the top of the list.

His goals for the future are also quite consistent with his spiritually based concern for others. Specifically, he wants to: "(1) advance the health status of individuals and the community; and (2) minister to the physical, spiritual, and emotional needs of people."

By doing for others before thinking of himself, this doctor has reached a high level of success, which he defines as "a sense of achievement, good reputation, and respect among peers, public, friends, and associates."

SPIRITUAL PRINCIPLE 7: It's Essential to Make a Total Commitment

A radical kind of highly demanding faith is the only kind that seems able to move mountains or propel anyone to the aeries of super success.

That kind of total commitment is what seems to characterize one of our most fascinating interviewees, a chief executive officer of a life insurance company. With an annual income of more than $200,000, he seems tailor-made to fit the image of the completely independent, self-made man. Yet he feels that the source of his success, although rooted in his own powers and gifts, ultimately transcends the mere human. In listing the reasons for his great achievements, he said:

"I have always been lucky.

"I seldom express rage.

"I have a great sense of humor.

"I don't remember slights against or hatred directed at me.

"I don't hate.

"I pray long and often."

He placed a star beside the last statement.

Even though his family was poor, he had a strong religious upbringing and strong moral support from his family in his climb toward success.

"I have always had good friends and loved ones surrounding me," he explained. "This has been a major influence on me!"

He went on to say, "I've been married 38 years to the only girl I ever dated. I'm very fortunate."

Now, although he possesses all the material trappings of success, he says his favorite activity is "preparing a Sunday school lesson for a very large adult Bible class." Also, when we asked him what books had greatly influenced him, he said, "the Bible, printed sermons, and poetry in general."

This man summed up his total spiritual commitment in this concluding statement: "I have always felt the presence of Jesus Christ in my life. I owe all to Him."

Donald Seibert of J. C. Penney has called his religious faith the "primary principle" in his business life. By this, he means his Christian commitment has provided an integrating force and principle that helps him set his priorities and order his relationships on the job more effectively.

That seems to sum up the attitudes of many of the successful religious people we surveyed. For them, faith is no guarantee of financial rewards or career achievements. Nor do they regard their religious commitment as some sort of pragmatic means to an earthly end. But their spiritual beliefs have certainly provided them with an emotional and spiritual underpinning as they've moved toward the promised land of worldly success.

Part II

THE
FRUITS OF
SUCCESS

CHAPTER

HOW DOES SUCCESS PAY OFF?

Once you've had a good opening night, you can't wait to do the next night. An initial success causes you to be more confident and pleased with yourself the next time around.

Ed McMahon, television host and actor

Does success guarantee financial rewards? Can money buy happiness? How about just enjoying your work—will that, in itself, increase your chances of happiness?

In this chapter, we'll look at these and similar questions, and we'll see how America's most successful people have responded to them. But first, an overview:

Sixty percent of our interviewees, on a scale of zero to 10, gave a rating of 5 or less when asked how much of a role the desire to make money had played in their success. Only 8 percent gave the top 9 or 10 ratings to money as a motive.

What does this mean? Simply that 92 percent of America's most successful people consider the desire to make money as only somewhat important or not important at all as a factor in their success.

This is ironic considering the income levels of those who responded. More than four out of five earn in excess of $50,000 annually; and 38 percent earn $100,000 or more each year! So you might say it's no wonder these achievers don't consider money that important—after all, they have plenty!

Still, personal satisfaction and happiness do seem to have much greater importance for these top achievers than do material considerations.

But our survey did give plenty of clear-cut, concrete information about the payoff of success. In short, our study told us a great deal about how success rewards those who make it to the top. What we discovered is that the payoff for success comes in two parts: (1) the material trappings and (2) the psychic or inner rewards.

THE MATERIAL TRAPPINGS OF SUCCESS

Try this personality profile:

"He's got a nice $50 watch but no boat. Saturday finds him working till six. He may not know a Vermeer from a velvet painting, but he could be an expert on the dry-cleaning business. He's a personable guy."

Who is he?

"He's America's typical millionaire," says *The Wall Street Journal,* in commenting on the research of Thomas Stanley, a marketing professor at Georgia State University in Atlanta. Stanley has studied the rich of America for the past 12 years.

In an article in the spring of 1985, the *Journal* reported: "The high-profile leisure class shows up as a minority in Mr. Stanley's research. Much more common is the owner of a small business—a string of dry-cleaning stores, hamburger

120

franchises, or travel-agency offices—who works long hours and doesn't have time for a vacation.

"They're boringly prudent in their spending. Only 1 in 10 owns a yacht, and a mere 1 in 20 owns a plane. Such collectibles as stamps, coins, precious metals, and art account for only 5 percent of their wealth. About half have second homes."

The *Journal's* report concludes by saying, "The key word, alas, is work. The rich are a painfully disciplined lot. But those 75-hour workweeks aren't in vain. Says Mr. Stanley: 'These are some of the happiest people in the world.' "

Our survey of successful men and women seems to agree on many points with Stanley's findings. But there are also some differences. Respondents in our study are not all millionaires—though as a group they do make a lot of money.

Specifically, 2 percent earned less than $20,000 per year; 13 percent were in the $20,000–$50,000 range; 45 percent had incomes between $50,000 and $100,000; 22 percent fell in the $100,000–$200,000 range; and an incredible 16 percent made more than $200,000 per year.

Obviously, these are very high incomes compared with what the average American earns. So, one result of success seems to be a relatively large income.

As we indicated in an earlier chapter, this finding clashes with another Gallup survey. In that poll, the average American indicated that an income of $37,000 per year should qualify someone as a success. But those who really are successful make a great deal more.

There are other material trappings that tend to accompany success. Specifically, our study revealed the following:

- Two out of three successful people own original paintings.
- Nearly half own antiques.

- Nearly 4 in 10 own a video cassette recorder.
- Thirty-five percent own two homes.
- More than three in 10 own three or more cars.
- Fifteen percent have a swimming pool in their backyard.
- Thirteen percent own a pool table.
- About one in 10 own either a motor boat or a jacuzzi.
- Five percent have a yacht.
- Two percent own a tennis court.
- One percent own paddle tennis courts.

Of course, we must keep a sense of perspective on the relationship between money, material goods, and success. Most of our top achievers felt that money wasn't that important in determining their level of success. Rather, high income and material luxuries were regarded as something that accompanied success, rather than caused it.

The peripheral nature of possessions came across loud and clear in the responses of a 78-year-old New England artist.

"Owing to the approaching Depression I had to finance myself through my last two years of college and did so by summer jobs and by buying and selling antiques," he recalled. "Right now, I consider myself to be well off as I own my own house, land (four acres), and car. Also, I have no mortgages or debts and can live very comfortably on what nowadays appears to be a rather small income [less than $20,000 per year].

"It has been said that if you live under your income, you are rich, and I believe that to be true. I have one son who is very successful and whose income is probably five or six times greater than mine. He has two daughters, both of whom have graduated from Harvard."

On a zero to 10 scale, we asked our respondents to rank

Figure 7-1
RELATIVE IMPORTANCE
OF VARIOUS "REWARDS"   (9 or 10 Rating)

Sense of personal worth, self-respect	**80%**
Recognition by one's peers	**58%**
Being able to contribute to society	**56%**
Approval by spouse	**46%**
Approval by parents	**22%**
Recognition by the public	**14%**

various items as being important or unimportant rewards of success. This artist gave an 8 rating to the importance of having enough money to buy or do anything; also, he awarded a more moderate 6 to the importance of owning expensive belongings.

But did he feel he had actually attained these two rewards?

To find out, we asked him to indicate the extent to which he had achieved the various rewards of success. He gave himself a 2 rating on each item.

It's important, however, to keep these individual responses in perspective. Only 3 percent of those surveyed considered expensive belongings, such as cars or homes, to be very important rewards of success. As a matter of fact, these material rewards ranked the lowest of all the categories. And less than 1 in 10 considered having the money to buy or do anything they wanted as very important. Personal power and social status were also at the bottom of the rankings, with only 4 percent of our respondents giving them top marks as rewards of success.

In line with this deemphasis on material possessions, a successful sculptor, whose income is in the $50,000–$100,000 range, says his formula for success has been: "Imagination, dedication, willingness to sacrifice or postpone material rewards, and generosity in giving the most one can to each project, without major concern for personal profit."

Yet on our scale of zero to 10, he gave rather high ratings of 7 for having money to buy or do anything and for owning expensive belongings. And he gave himself a 7 for having actually achieved those rewards.

Material possessions do comprise a significant backdrop in the lives of our top achievers; but the money motive isn't the main force that drives them. Nor are worldly possessions the rewards they value most as a consequence of their success.

Furthermore, even though blatant materialism may be a major problem in American culture today, our study reveals that materialism is mostly a peripheral side benefit for those who make it to the top.

So if money isn't the key payoff for high achievement, what *is* important to the successful?

To answer this question, we must turn to some of the less tangible rewards of success.

THE PSYCHIC REWARDS OF SUCCESS

Whereas money and expensive belongings rank toward the bottom of the rewards of success that our top achievers value, the less tangible psychic rewards occupy a much higher position.

For example, a sense of personal worth and self-respect is the most important reward of success, according to our successful people. An impressive 80 percent of them considered this to be of such supreme importance that they gave it a 9 or 10 rating.

On the other hand, considerably fewer—60 percent—felt very strongly that they had actually achieved this feeling of personal worth and self-respect.

Generally speaking, a pattern emerged in our responses: our respondents extolled certain psychic values as all-important rewards of success but often expressed considerable uncertainty about whether they had actually obtained those rewards.

Fifty-eight percent considered having recognition by one's peers as very important (i.e., worth a 9 or 10 rating). But only 47 percent felt strongly that they had actually gained this recognition. In a related finding, it's interesting that 14 percent gave a 9 or 10 rating to public recognition as an extremely important reward of success. But a larger number, 26 percent, felt they had actually achieved this recognition.

An altruistic factor came through clearly: 56 percent thought that being able to contribute to society was a very important reward of success. They thought such contributions would give them significant inner satisfaction. Only 37 percent were convinced they had made such a contribution.

Although many indicated they had fallen short of fully achieving the most important benefits of success, there were other rewards they felt they had achieved. One of these was approval from a spouse. Nearly half said the approval of their spouse was extremely important to them; even more, 66 percent, indicated that they had received such strong approval.

In reporting on Professor Thomas Stanley's survey of American millionaires, *The Wall Street Journal* uncovered some similar sentiments. The *Journal* said of the millionaires,

"They are quite generous . . . in giving credit to their wives. Almost all American millionaires are men, and they tend to have what Stanley calls 'Tammy Wynette' wives. The wives 'stand by their men,' from the lean early days to the good life years later."

Also, parental approval was considered very important by 22 percent of the top achievers in our survey, and two thirds of our interviewees felt that they had received such approval.

Because many of our respondents had relatively good relationships with their parents, it's natural that they would continue to value their early family influences and admire their parents. Such was the case with one corporate executive. In advising young people, she said, "Do not expect material rewards, but put top value on societal long-term improvement. Have a world view."

The emphasis on intellectual and intangible values in her life began quite early and contributed, she feels, to her broad background.

As a child, she was raised in an academic environment, where "financial and material gain were not the most important values. An advantage of an academic upbringing is the independent attitude one can have—you're not tied to an economic or social class. This possibly results in a more objective outlook that makes you an observer of society as a whole. And you have little pressure to conform with goals of a particular group of peers. You become competitive with your own standards, not competitive against others."

As might be expected, this woman gave low marks to the material trappings of success (e.g., money, expensive belongings, social status, personal power). In contrast, she valued the more abstract rewards of achievement, such as personal worth and self-respect.

Perhaps the most radical and inspiring statements in favor of the psychic rewards of success came from those who had made their mark in the arts.

One poet said, "I try not to encourage too many into a life of writing. So few seem well suited, and the course is a long one, full of pitfalls. The rewards—especially in poetry—are special and hard to define: The joy of doing it right, doing it first, *getting it!* Making music with language."

On the other hand, this man offered a kind of mixed bag when we asked him to describe the evidence of his personal success. He responded: "Personal gratification. The regard of my peers. Fame. Happiness."

So the evidence strongly suggests that it is *not* mainly the material trappings of success that spur achievers to great heights. Rather, the most significant factors are the more subjective rewards, such as a sense of personal worth and self-respect and approval of peers and loved ones.

Yet we still haven't dealt with the bottom-line payoff of success: how happy and satisfied are those at the top?

WILL SUCCESS MAKE YOU HAPPY?

A 76-year-old New England lawyer told us, "I know this sounds bigheaded, but I have been successful in a highly competitive environment. Yet I have been both successful *and* happy in my family life."

Part of this man's happiness stems from his career achievements; part from his rewarding family experience; and part from his active, inquiring intellectual interests.

"I started (literally) in debt—and now, I am wealthy," he explained. "I have a wonderful wife and five successful children in various occupations. My health is now only fair, but my mind—thanks be to whatever may cause it—seems to be clear. And I am still influential for a man my age. I am still interested in many things I read about."

He concluded with a good-natured flourish: "Thanks for giving me an opportunity to tell you how good I am!"

Like this attorney, slightly more than half of those in our survey said they were very happy. Yet the rest said they were only fairly happy or not happy at all. Why wouldn't a successful individual be very happy? Or, to put the question in a broader, more positive way: what are the ingredients for achieving success *and* happiness.

One type of answer comes from a geotechnical engineer in the Southwest, who said, "My greatest apprehension about retirement is that I may have too little responsibility. I am trying to establish some responsibilities that I hope will keep me usefully productive."

As he nears the end of his career, considerations other than money have become the biggest source of anxieties for this man. "I have no financial worries about retirement," he noted. "But I think a person just has to keep on being (and feeling) useful, or there's no point to life. My main regret, in retrospect, is that I did not spend more time with my children and get to know them better. Somehow, I failed to inspire them with any drive for obtaining higher education, and this has, I believe, hindered their own successes and happiness."

A professor at a large midwestern university also indicated that he had experienced some twinges of uncertainty about the meaning of his career achievements. On paper, he has everything going for him. As he puts it, "A doctor's degree from a top university; a full professorship at a major university at 36; a distinguished teaching award; offices in national organizations; many publications that have been used widely."

But in describing the daily nature of his work, he revealed the tremendous, frustrating pressures of his packed schedule.

He said, "I teach undergraduate and graduate classes, have graduate advisees, write professional books and articles, give presentations at professional meetings, fill out all sorts of reports, and attend silly meetings."

This professor's evaluation is a microcosm of the feelings expressed by many of our other top achievers: "One must *be able* in most instances to be successful; but I think there is a lot of serendipity, dumb luck in life. I'm learning slowly that it's more important to be happy, loved, healthy, contented, than to be successful. I wish that people could switch careers two, three, four times. I wish we had more time for fun and less time consumed by the need to earn a living. I think we are losing more and more personal freedom and becoming increasingly totalitarian bureaucratic.

"Rather than all the trappings of success, I wish I had about 30 acres of ground out in the country where there is some peace and quiet and I could play with my grandchildren.

"Success isn't all it's cracked up to be," he said.

But even with such serious ponderings about the meaning of his career and life, this professor showed he hasn't lost his sense of humor. When we asked him if his family owned any luxury items, such as a second home or a swimming pool, he said, "I must be a failure after all! How about two tennis rackets?"

Many listed in Marquis' *Who's Who In America* revealed that they are not completely satisfied with many aspects of their lives. Yet the overwhelming majority of respondents are more satisfied than dissatisfied. Also, they tend to be more satisfied about specific aspects of their lives than the general public.

Ninety percent said they were more satisfied than dissatisfied with their personal lives (they gave themselves at least a 6 on the satisfaction scale). In a survey we did among the general public, a smaller number (79 percent) indicated they were satisfied with their personal lives.

As far as material things are concerned, half said they were very satisfied with their standard of living, and 92 percent indicated they were at least fairly satisfied. Again, a significantly lower 78 percent of the general public indicated satisfaction with their standard of living.

Satisfaction with their home situation was also a positive factor among our top achievers. More than half said they got along very well with their spouses; about half got along very well with their children; and half were very satisfied in general with their family life. More than 8 in 10 were at least fairly satisfied in these family areas. Almost the same number in the general public were happy with their family lives, according to our survey.

As for their jobs, 48 percent of our achievers were very satisfied at work, and 86 percent were at least fairly satisfied. Among the general public, a lower figure, 70 percent, were satisfied with their careers.

The responses of a professor at a southern university illustrate the often complex mixture of fulfillment, uncertainty, and ongoing challenge that top achievers experience on the job.

"You might have gotten at some factors by asking what are the greatest fears," he said. "I fear increasing isolation from others, coming in part from success. Some motivation for success comes from the desire to leave behind some work that will survive—a search for a conditional immortality. In my case, this means writing books, but in other cases, it might be building a corporation or business, leading political or social changes, etc.

"The late R. P. Blackmoor (writer, critic, Princeton professor) said that you can have a happy life or you can do good work, but not both. Is this borne out in your survey?"

The most accurate answer to this provocative question is sometimes yes, sometimes no. But we might also answer him with these remarks from the chief executive of a high-technology research company:

"Married nearly four decades ago, my wife and I have three children and two grandsons, and we expect more grandchildren. We're fortunate to agree on rather high standards of self-discipline and achievement for ourselves and our children.

"We have always enjoyed our children and especially now enjoy their company as adults. Most important of all, we believe that we have been able to transfer our values to our offspring. That's one of the best rewards possible, especially since my wife and I both have our own careers."

This executive indicated that he's extremely satisfied with his standard of living and the way his education has prepared him. Yet his life is apparently not all a bed of roses: he said he's just fairly, as opposed to very, happy. Also, he's only somewhat satisfied with his personal life, his job, and the way he's able to spend his free time.

How top achievers enjoy their free time provides some interesting food for thought. Only 39 percent of those we surveyed gave this area a satisfaction rating of 9 or 10. On the other hand, a much more substantial 82 percent were at least somewhat satisfied with the way they spend their free time; that is, they gave this point a rating of at least 6. A comparable percentage of the general public, 78 percent, told us in another survey that they were satisfied with the way they spent their free hours.

What do these responses mean? From general statistics and individual surveys we've examined, it seems that most top achievers do enjoy vacations and free hours with friends and loved ones. Yet their schedules are so packed with commitments and pressures that they don't get as much time off as they would like. Also, when they do have free time, they find it hard to wind down and tend to be preoccupied with work concerns. Perhaps, then, this brings us full circle, back to the comment from the southern professor who wondered whether you have to choose between having a happy life and doing good work.

In another thoughtful response, a mechanical engineer told us that he is very happy with his life. In part, he feels that the evidence of success and rewards of success should include plenty of money and expensive belongings. True to his words, he owns a yacht, antiques, a motor boat, and original paintings and earns close to $100,000 a year.

But for this man, there's clearly more to achievement than money. He remarked, "To me, being a success is mostly a personal thing. I measure it mainly by how I feel about myself after having made some kind of achievement. Unless I have really deserved an honor, I mistrust it.

"One should always try to accomplish as much as one's abilities will allow. Do not try to equal the achievement of another. Always seek to help others in a positive way—sometimes by example, other times by advice or definite guidance or material assistance.

"Happiness is a by-product, derived only from a sense of well-being resulting from making your life count for something worthwhile."

Apparently, this achiever has come to terms with the meaning of success because his responses reveal an inner peace uncharacteristic of others we surveyed. For example, on issues that are closer to home, he gave 10 ratings to his personal life, family life, standard of living, and education. In contrast, only about half of our other respondents answered with such enthusiastic satisfaction on these points.

Also, whereas many others indicated a definite dissatisfaction with the way things are going in this country, our engineer gave this item an 8 rating.

Finally, the concrete reasons for his satisfaction are best summed up in his personal formula for success.

"First, seek the finest formal education possible in one's field.

"Second, establish a goal that at first seems beyond achievement;

"Third, work extra hard and effectively, and then work some more;

"Fourth, always try to help others;

"Fifth, place strong belief in God; and

"Sixth, marry a spouse who believes in your goals and principles."

Many times, inner satisfaction and happiness appear inextricably intertwined with the degree to which people *savor* the actual process of working. In other words, they don't just work to finish a task or scramble to make it to the top—rather, they enjoy practically every detail, at every step along the way.

In this vein, a research scientist told us, "I enjoy the work I do very much. The maximum satisfaction I get from my career is the pleasure I derive from this work—both the satisfaction of my curiosity in my own work and in reading the research of others."

He also indicated a strong belief in luck as an important ingredient in his success. In fact, he gave luck a 10 rating, and he awarded a 9 rating to the statement, "I was just born lucky."

Finally, consider this scientist's formula for success: "Being properly prepared, but not being swayed by others' opinions. Good PR and being in the right place at the right time."

Much of the satisfaction and happiness experienced by our top achievers have also come from the quality of the relationships they have with their children. For example, a retired officer in the transportation industry says, "I am quite pleased with the way my children have progressed. All three were merit scholars and have graduated with honors from undergraduate and professional schools."

He goes on to explain, "One son is now a neurologist, and the other is a lawyer for a large New York law firm. My daughter is a lawyer for the federal government and has received special recognition in her department. My five grandchildren are healthy, intelligent, and doing well. At my age, it is extremely important to me to see young people coming along who can keep our nation strong."

Even though some respondents had equally resounding statements of happiness and contentment, most were more equivocal. For example, a midwestern teacher told us, "I am near the end of my career, and I still don't know how one determines success by external measures. My career has not been perfect or all fulfilling. It has been productive and interesting. I have won some and lost some."

He did say that he had further goals in life, but when asked to define them, he was somewhat uncertain: "Not clear—perhaps one more career of note," he responded.

Like nearly half of our other achievers, he rated himself as fairly happy. He seemed concerned about his income (between $20,000 and $50,000 a year) and graded himself poorly on his ability to make money, own expensive belongings, and buy or do anything. Still he rated the desire for money as only a negligible factor in his success.

Yet this man is far from financially troubled—his family owns two homes and three or more cars, and he lives rather well on his income.

Finally, one bittersweet comment from the head of a department in library management highlights the trouble many top achievers have in evaluating the payoff of their own success.

"I have tried to answer honestly, but [your] questions presuppose a self-knowledge that few have," he said. "Success, however measured, is always the result of a combination of factors, not easily susceptible to analysis. I see people around me, moreover, whose success seems to have come about through factors far different from my own. For some of these people, I have disdain or contempt, but I cannot deny their success."

So, in the last analysis, how does success pay off?

In monetary terms, the answer is "quite well." Successful people have a substantial amount of money at their disposal, with 83 percent of them making more than $50,000 a year and many possessing such material trappings of success as extra homes, cars, artwork, and other luxury items. In addition, our respondents have gained significant public and professional recognition for their achievements—thus giving them higher social status than the general public.

But large numbers of our *Who's Who* respondents downplay the importance of material rewards. Clearly, they need something else to justify their drive to the top and to fulfill their needs after they get there.

In short, most top achievers strive for inner affirmations, like a sense of personal worth and self-respect. Just as important, they value—and, in many cases, are still desperately seeking—those two elusive benefits that have tantalized humanity in every era, namely, great happiness and satisfaction. They want to be able to say, as Cervantes did, ". . . come what will come, I am satisfied."

CHAPTER

THE HYPERTIME DIMENSION OF HIGH ACHIEVEMENT

A formula for success: Being willing to learn new things; being able to assimilate new information quickly; and being able to get along with and work with other people.

Sally Ride, astronaut

"Oh dear! Oh dear! I shall be too late!"

So muttered the White Rabbit as he pulled a watch out of his waistcoat pocket and scurried off to Wonderland. It's the sort of sentiment that we hear or feel every day of our lives as we confront deadlines and responsibilities.

We live in a society dominated and defined by time. What we get done, how much money we make, and what we contribute to our culture depend largely on how well we use the 24 hours available to us each day. Those who are most successful in life are the people who can enter another time dimension—those who can accomplish more in a lifetime than the rest of us.

But for most successful people, wrestling with the demands of time can be a formidable challenge. One leading teacher from the Northeast told us, "I was on leave for one year in order to teach in Alaska. While I was there, I visited a satellite tracking station. As you might imagine, there were rooms filled with complicated equipment which was being used to record the movement of satellites orbiting in space. I was impressed with the immensity and complexity of the project."

But one of those rooms made this woman feel uneasy: "This was a room full of clocks that showed the time all over the world. As each second passed, the hand on every clock jumped forward, and the time flashed in glowing green digits beneath each clock.

"Being confronted in this way by the relentless passing of time started to depress me. I was too aware that each passing second was lost to me forever. I was very glad to leave that room because it had begun to take on a nightmarish quality for me," she concluded.

This woman has risen to a prominent position in education and become a leader in religious activities in one of the nation's largest urban centers. But she still has to fight feeling intimidated by the many demands of her life.

She is not alone. Time pressure plagues many of the other top achievers we interviewed. They generally agree with R. Alec Mackenzie, who explains in his classic book *The Time Trap* that time is a unique, ever-wasting resource:

"It cannot be accumulated like money or stockpiled like raw materials. We are forced to spend it whether we choose to or not, and at a fixed rate of 60 seconds every minute. It cannot be turned on and off like a machine or replaced like a man. It is irretrievable."[1]

---

[1] R. Alec Mackenzie, *The Time Trap* (New York: McGraw-Hill, 1975), p. 2.

Yet most successful individuals manage to rise above the pressure of limited time and demanding deadlines. And they get more done.

They seem to enter another dimension of reality—a hypertime dimension, if you will—that opens the way to peak achievement. Most people pack one life into their 70 or so years. Top achievers seem to cram in two, three, or more.

What exactly do they do with their time—and what can we learn from them?

We and others have uncovered the following findings about how super successful people use their time:

They Work Long Hours

The typical executive puts in a 63-hour workweek (53 hours in the office and 10 at home), according to a Daniel Howard study. This survey revealed that a few top achievers work as many as 90 or 100 hours a week.

Almost 6 out of 10 Are Involved in Volunteer Activities

And they're not passive about it. Our successful respondents said they average 3.1 hours per week on volunteer activities—a much greater amount of time than that spent by the general public. Specifically, 43 percent said they donate time to help the poor, disadvantaged, or needy. Another 31 percent donate time to religious work. And 72 percent have written a letter to a political official or signed a political petition. Some respondents spend 20 or more hours on nonwork projects.

For example, one corporate chief executive who earns more than $200,000 a year said he spends 20 hours a week on volunteer activities. He serves as chairman of a college board, works for the Salvation Army, teaches a regular Bible study, and serves on eight civic projects.

The overwhelming majority of our respondents are not satisfied with pursuing just one set of interests. They love the tremendous diversity of activities available to them, and they try to pursue as many as possible. Their great natural abilities and time management capacities enable them to taste success and fulfillment in many areas, both on the job and off. And apparently, the more they sample the flavors of life, the more they want.

More Than 7 out of 10 Are Currently Reading a Book

On average, our high achievers read 19 books a year, or more than 1 book every three weeks—9 works of fiction and 10 of nonfiction. The median was 12 books a year, 6 of fiction and 6 of nonfiction. This indicates that the half who read the most read extremely heavily, so that the average is well above the median. In fact, 19 percent of our respondents said they read 26 or more books a year, again, almost evenly divided between fiction and nonfiction.

Although many of our successful individuals listed various hobbies and family events as their favorite leisure activities, reading was by far one of the most popular pastimes. This shouldn't be surprising—as we've seen, there is a positive correlation between success and reading. How do achievers approach their personal reading programs?

Donald V. Seibert, the former chairman of the board of
J. C. Penney, had this to say in his book *The Ethical Executive:*

"I can't give you any absolute rules about what you should
read to succeed in business. But let me suggest a few guidelines
that may be helpful in enhancing your successful image. First
of all, let's consider how much time you should spend in reading
peripheral matters each day—i.e., not business correspondence
or other required on-the-job reading, but such things as newspapers, magazines, and books.

"I spend a couple of hours every day on this 'outside' reading. If I'm traveling by train or airplane, I often read and
scan this sort of material from departure to arrival. When I'm
on vacation, I devote two or three hours each day to general
reading. . . . The main point here is that it's important to do
some significant amount of outside reading: Don't skimp on
it!"[2]

Eight out of 10 Belong to Clubs and Organizations

These include every imaginable kind of organization, including professional and social clubs, country clubs, and athletic facilities.

One reason successful people are able to accomplish so
much is that, first, like Templeton and Seibert, they don't

---

[2]   Donald V. Seibert and William Proctor, *The Ethical Executive* (New York: Simon & Schuster, 1984), p. 112.

141

waste a minute and, second, they do an excellent job of split-second scheduling.

Successful people don't squander their time on unproductive activities. For example, they spend few hours watching television. When we asked respondents how many hours they watched television in a typical day, we obtained the following information.

Percentage of those surveyed	Number of TV hours
11%	0
43	1–1:59
28	2–2:59
8	3
4	more than 3
6	no response

On the average, our respondents watched television 1.5 hours per day. In contrast, the average television-owning household spends an average of more than seven hours in front of the tube each day, according to the *Nielsen Report*.

What are our top achievers most likely to be doing while the rest of us are staring at the TV screen? The answer: working hard.

As we've seen, when our respondents were asked to rate the factors that contributed most to their success, two responses topped the list, with a rating of 9 or 10: the ability to get things done, which got 68 percent; and hard work and diligence, with 67 percent.

Clearly, these factors relate to the effective use of time. Successful people focus on accomplishment and achievement, and they have a superior understanding of what they are capable of finishing within a given time period. They place a high value on completing what they begin, and they believe in getting the job done through consistent hard work.

Now, let's see how some of these time-related skills are employed effectively in practice. One 41-year-old executive vice president of a major corporation said he would give this advice to young people entering his field:

"Maximize your time, which is your scarcest asset. If time is used well, other rewards will follow. Build a firm technical foundation early in your career, even at the sacrifice of status or financial rewards. Don't give up in the face of adversity. Take moderate risks and remember that most success comes from hard work and self-discipline, not luck."

Figure 8-1
EXPERIENCE IN CHOSEN FIELD (9 or 10 Rating)

Ability to get things done	**68%**
Hard work, diligence	**67%**
Ambition, desire to get ahead	**51%**
Ability to motivate subordinates	**41%**
Luck, timing, being in the right place, right time	**38%**
Respect for peers	**37%**
Organizational ability	**35%**
Special talent in chosen field	**33%**

His own life reflects this conviction that success depends on wise use of time. Born the eldest of four children, he grew up in what he considers a below-average financial situation.

As a boy he was able to attend excellent schools because he worked hard in part-time jobs and in his academic tasks. As a result, he graduated in the top third of his class in high school and college. After college, he attended graduate school.

This businessperson now earns more than $200,000 a year and describes his work as involving the following areas: "leveraged buyouts, usually by employees; labor negotiations; strategic and marketing planning; international trade and trade finance."

For a young man, he has already achieved outstanding success in a field that requires at least three key qualities: (1) highly specialized knowledge, (2) a reputation built on honesty and sound thinking, and (3) a capacity for hard work.

He says that possessing the following abilities has enabled him to achieve his success:

- The ability to work with people and to understand their problems from *their* point of view.
- The ability to work quickly and accurately to satisfy customer needs.
- The ability to structure deals and transactions where everyone wins.
- The ability to put people at ease.
- Integrity in personal relationships. "Always be fair, never cheat."

Clearly, this man does not waste time. Yet he has had many extracurricular and intellectual interests outside his chosen field, both in high school and college. He was a team captain in high school and still enjoys sports. Running and racquetball are two of his present favorite pastimes. Furthermore, like many of the other achievers we interviewed, he donates time to helping poor, disadvantaged, or needy people.

Reading is another activity he enjoys. He read 26 books in the past year (20 of them fiction).

When he was asked about his future goals, he didn't mention business at all. Instead, he said his goals are "too many to list, but the key is to continuously stay on a new learning curve. Also, I want to leverage past experience into scaling new heights and meeting new challenges."

This dynamic individual is able to do a considerable amount of reading, participate in sports, and respond to the needs of society, as well as work hard at his career. Like many of our other successes, he wants it all—and he's willing to cram plenty of extras into his daily schedule to savor his life to the maximum. He practices what he preaches.

Another of our human-whirlwind respondents, a 52-year-old Texas businessman, has found time for prodigious amounts of volunteer activity. Among the service organizations to which he donates time, he lists: the Salvation Army, Boy Scouts of America, a clean city commission, and an inner-city revitalization project.

How does he find the time? He says that he possesses an ability to boil complex matters down to their essence. In other words, he doesn't jump into each new project without thinking. Rather, he mulls it over, examines it from every angle, and determines first whether it has sufficient merit for him to get involved. If it does have merit, he then determines how he can contribute most effectively, given the other demands on his time.

In short, this businessperson has learned to plan in advance and to simplify his commitments so that he maximizes every minute of his time. He has truly entered the hypertime dimension that paves the way to high achievement.

Another of those we interviewed, a professor of physics, is committed to the following professional associations: Fellow of the Royal Society of Chemistry, Institute of Physics, Royal Astronomical Society, American Physical Society, American Association of the Advancement of Science, and the Royal

Institution of Great Britain. He also attends meetings of Mensa, the high-IQ society.

But for this man, as well as for virtually all of our other success stories, the time devoted to work comes first. He says, "I am very dedicated to my profession, and I work constantly (96 to 100 hours per week)."

Yet, like many other achievers, this professor makes sure he devotes time to other interests and responsibilities that he feels make him a whole person.

"I'm concerned about cultivating my family and cultural life, with outside interests including music and church activities," he says. "Ideals, integrity, and refinement mean very much to me."

His favorite pastimes are being with his family, talking with friends, reading, playing music (he's adept at more than one instrument), and painting. He is presently reading four books and has read 38 books within the past year. Also, he enjoys creating works of art. In addition to all these activities, he devotes four hours a week to volunteer activities in his church.

Underlying this professor's approach to time is a philosophy of life that seems to give him a certain equanimity under pressure. Advising young people thinking of entering his field, he says, "Do not compromise ideals; maintain integrity and intellectual curiosity and diversity, regard your profession as a service to be taken seriously, but yourself not too seriously."

One of the best summaries of time management came from a corporate executive who told us that, to succeed, "An inquiring mind—that is, having a lively and broad-ranging set of interests—is fundamental. Then, you need an ability to organize your time and that of others to attain clearly recognized goals with a minimum of distraction and wasted effort.

"In short, those who want to maximize their achievements need an ability to distinguish between what is important and what is not important.

"Finally, you have to be able to persuade other people if you hope to accomplish much in this world.

"These qualities and skills are what it takes to succeed—and they are even more important than hard work, per se."

Many of our successful people have developed this ability to separate the trivial from the essential. They know how to recognize and focus on priorities. Then when they find goals and activities that warrant their attention, they turn into radical activists.

Part III

THE
FUTURE
SUCCESS
STORY

CHAPTER

A LOOK AT TOMORROW
BY THE TOP ACHIEVERS
OF TODAY

In the reporting business, you have to know your stuff. When that camera is live, you have to be prepared for it.

Morton Dean, television anchor and correspondent

As we've seen, the nation's top achievers make excellent use of their daily time—a fact that adds up to super achievement when they reach the prime of life.

Part of making the most efficient use of each day involves planning wisely for the future. So, as might be expected, successful people set their goals carefully.

Furthermore, they have a broad perspective on the future. They sense where they *and* society are most likely to be heading. They know that what they are able to accomplish depends, at least in part, on the overall movement of the culture in which they operate. Top achievers tend to be forward-looking, positive thinkers even as they approach retirement. But, before we get into specifics, it's helpful to consider the age ranges of the people we're talking about. Six percent of our respondents were younger than 40; 12 percent were 40 to 49; 30 percent were 50 to 59; 36 percent were 60 to 69; and 14 percent were 70 or older. (The median age was well into the 50s.)

Yet even at this level of maturity, our achievers were still setting goals: two thirds said there are further goals they want to achieve in life. Furthermore, they listed a wide variety of specific personal goals. For example, about 10 percent wanted to write books. Others said they wanted to get out of debt, advance their career still further, learn to love their spouse again, spend more time with their family, further some religious cause, or increase their knowledge in some way. One attorney aspired to write a "great literary novel."

These people continue to be active thinkers and actors as they have been all their lives—and they don't intend to slow down as they get older.

But the personal, self-oriented level of goal setting is just one way these top achievers approach the future. They are equally concerned with the state of American society and the international situation, and how they could contribute to improving things on the social and political scene.

In fact, about 10 percent indicated that they wanted to improve society in some way. One man wanted to "assist the Hopi Indians." Another wanted to address the "overarching problems of today's world—food, births, peace." And a doctor wanted to help "advance knowledge in my speciality and disseminate the information to help improve the state of medicine in the world."

One of the motives that drives these achievers to work hard for society is that, as a group, they are worried about the drift of American culture. This general concern was reflected in a satisfaction index included in the *Who's Who* survey. Respondents were asked to rate (from zero to 10) how satisfied they were with "the way things are going in this country at this time."

Only 5 percent said they were at the 9 or 10 level of satisfaction with the state of the nation. Slightly more than half indicated they were at least somewhat satisfied, giving a rating of 6 or above. The general public, by the way, responded similarly; 52 percent said they were satisfied to some degree with the general drift of the country.

The reasons for dissatisfaction with the direction of our society are quite varied. But often, the factors that most concern our achievers have some deep personal meaning. The following eight key problems emerged from our study.

PROBLEM 1: Discrimination

The strongest statements about discrimination came from people who had experienced it. Two high achievers discuss the subject—one who overcame prejudice and one who is still struggling with the problem.

"As an ambitious, black female, I was subjected to more than my share of racism and sexism," says a prominent college professor. "With the help of others—white and black—I learned to rise above the discrimination and to give full attention to teaching and research."

She explains her primary sources of strength this way: "My very supportive spouse was particularly important in helping me to reach my career goals."

Yet, help didn't come only from her personal relationships. "The nation's adoption of affirmative action policies has been helpful during the past 10 years," she says.

This woman has worked hard to achieve international recognition as a scholar in her field. She had no time for extracurricular activities in college because she had to work part time. While she was growing up, her family's income was below average although both her parents had attended college and her father went to graduate school.

But that's all behind her now. Her current family income

is between $100,000 and $200,000 a year, and she's generally quite satisfied with her family and occupational life. This professor also advises young people to be sure that their educational preparation is thorough. Her personal goal is to write more books in her field.

On the whole, then, this woman has moved beyond earlier discrimination, though she's still not happy with the state of the country.

Another college professor is even less sanguine about discrimination in the country and in her personal life. After giving a 4 rating to her satisfaction with the way things are going in the country, she states: "I feel handicapped in my profession because my employer flagrantly violates the antidiscrimination laws." She laments further, "The courts have so ruled, but no one enforces the laws."

How is she discriminated against? "All 'professional plums' go to the men and so does most of the budget, despite the Equal Pay Act."

This woman makes a substantial income, in the high five figures, and she has many of the material trappings of success. Also, she says she was fairly happy when she was growing up, and she seems to have had an intellectually stimulating childhood: she read much more than her peers, and both her parents went to college. Also, her family income as she grew up was above average.

Yet now, she says her life is "not too happy," and she's especially dissatisfied with her job, giving it only a rating of 1 on our scale of zero to 10. In short, she feels frustrated in her work and "unable to use" her education. An early financial advantage and a good education didn't save her from the sexism that now frustrates her. In an effort to escape this situation, she's currently working on another Ph.D. in order to change fields.

Discrimination, then, presents a nebulous picture for the

future. Some have noted progress, but others feel our society has a long way to go.

PROBLEM 2: Society's Responsiveness to Social Problems

An attorney with a sensitivity for those less fortunate than himself advises young people not to enter his field "if you're not an intellectual with compassion for society."

And his feelings spill over into his politics. A politically active person who is obviously committed to governmental social programs, this man was deeply disappointed that Walter Mondale wasn't elected president. He speculates that Mondale lost because "he was not charismatic or telegenic."

In highlighting his deep sense of social concern, he extols the leadership of the most visible spokesmen for Democratic social causes: "Hopefully, historians will teach our kids and grandchildren that at my party's convention, three great speeches were given by Fritz [Mondale], Jesse [Jackson], and Mario [Cuomo]."

He's obviously not a fan of the incumbent Republican administration: he gave a 4 rating to his feelings of satisfaction with the way things are currently going in the country. On the personal level, he says he's just fairly happy, mostly because he's going through a "friendly divorce."

On the other hand, he notes that he's usually very happy. And he gives the highest rating of 10 to his satisfaction with his job and his children. But other aspects of his life, including his free time and personal life in general, get low to middling ratings.

This man, of course, represents only one personal and political point of view. But many others agree that our nation still faces profound problems with the disadvantaged—even though some offer quite different solutions.

One conservative Republican, for example, told us that he was worried about what seemed to be an increasing number of "street people" and seriously deprived families in his area. But his twofold solution was quite different from that of the Mondale supporter:

"First, offer more vocational education for those who can't make it through a more rigorous academic route to college and graduate school. Second, work out a system to put the unemployed and poor people together with the jobs that haven't been filled. Work, not welfare, is the answer!"

PROBLEM 3: Maintaining Strong Family Life

A number of our respondents indicated that they think a productive and happy future for our culture depends on the development of strong families. One doctor, who grew up in a family with a below-average income, said both his parents had only a grade school education. While he was in high school he had to work one to two hours, evenings and Saturdays, shining shoes and sweeping floors in his father's small barber and beauty shop. Throughout college he worked summers as a busboy and waiter in resorts.

But even though financial concerns kept him busy while he was growing up, he developed a deep concern about the place of the family in society.

"Values seem to be changing from greater emphasis on family and social needs in previous generations, to personal and career goals in the present generation," he complained. "America needs a new stimulus to reestablish its leadership in productivity and social progress."

And he apparently feels that strong families should provide a large part of that stimulus. In particular, he's concerned about parents' failure to regulate the values promulgated on

156

television: "I believe that TV in America is on the whole detrimental to youth. Hollywood seriously distorts morality."

When he was growing up, this doctor got along very well with both his parents, one sister, and "several cousins who lived close by." His fondest memories of high school and college focused on family outings to the beach. And he still enjoys vacationing with family—now as the head of his own.

The neighborhood in which his family lived also exercised a profound influence on this man. He found role models and other influential individuals there, including some very bright neighborhood friends who challenged his goals."

He grew up in a family *and* in an extended family, in a world where cousins and friends and the family doctor were a big part of life, too.

His advice to aspiring doctors is consistent with his pro-family emphasis: "Try to develop your career *in a slow and steady manner, allowing for your personal and family needs and growth.*"

PROBLEM 4: Need for Instant Gratification

Seeing a difficult task through is a key capacity that many of our top achievers cite as crucial to their success. Yet some of them fear children today aren't learning to stick with tasks to completion. These achievers are worried that today's youngsters seem less able than older generations to persevere through difficulties.

One of our top achievers, a research scientist who makes close to $100,000 a year, summarized the problem rather colorfully:

"One of my big concerns is *instant gratification:*

A. Instant teas, coffee, oats, solutions.
B. Examine a model airplane kit, 1940s versus 1980s.
   1. 1940s:
      a. Hundreds of parts.
      b. Requires patience and precision.
   2. 1980s:
      a. Few parts.
      b. Requires 15 minutes and glue.
C. Watch a child with a TV tuner. They give every channel 30 seconds to grab and hold them. It's a matter of instant pleasure."

This man learned early to be patient and wait for results. But he's concerned that children now don't develop qualities and skills that have been vital to him in his life and work.

Patience, precision, a willingness to be different, and a strong sense of self—these are key qualities that have enabled this researcher, as he puts it, to (1) avoid the pitfall of fads, (2) plug away, and (3) stay with a *basic* line of research." This approach has resulted in his producing what he sees as a *"significant body* of work."

No instant gratification for this man. He takes life slowly, easily, and deliberately. He savors the process of achievement, even as he moves to greater heights in his career.

PROBLEM 5: Quality of Education

Nearly everyone we surveyed highly valued a good education, and many were concerned about what they saw as questionable trends in American education. But not everyone agreed on what those negative trends are and what can be done to correct the situation.

A psychologist said that he himself hadn't been the best candidate for college. He was a "brittle diabetic" who had to weigh his food, and colleges didn't want him in their dorms or cafeterias. He also hadn't done well in high school, mostly because he didn't like the courses, spent too much time on athletics, and read all the time. But he did make it to college and managed to graduate in the top 10th of his class.

He gives his college education a perfect 10 for preparing him well for life and for his career.

This psychologist advises young people who want to enter his field to study in various universities in different areas of the United States and abroad. He reasons that "too many people do all of their work at a school like Stanford. They are so shallow because they haven't been anywhere."

His proposed reforms include this advice: "Develop schools of professional entertainment in colleges. Stop bringing kids into college who can't read and will never graduate. Train your intellectual athletes there for the *pros.*"

Other respondents also made negative comments. A professor remarked about academic life as follows:

"Unfortunately, too much is a product of the buddy system, of intellectual dishonesty, and of manipulation of 'higher ups.' Ethics are missing."

When he was attending school, he recalls, "Deans and professors furnished negative role models, which made me want to do better than they."

Yet this professor hasn't given up on the system entirely, for he says he aspires to become a dean or college president as a next step up the career ladder. Somewhat surprisingly, he even advises young people to consider education as a career, in spite of the politics.

As valid as these criticisms of our educational system may be, it's important not to forget one telling statistic. When asked

"Did you ever have a teacher or teachers who made you enthusiastic about a particular subject?", 89 percent of our successful people answered *yes*. This figure is an overwhelming affirmation of the influence that teachers have had in the past—and undoubtedly will *continue* to have in the future.

In this regard, consider the approach of another teacher we interviewed who seemed to have it all—many career accomplishments, the recognition of his peers, a strong sense of personal worth, and an extremely satisfying home life. Yet this has not been quite sufficient for this man.

Even though he's in his late 50s, he keeps pushing to realize further goals, namely, "to address some of the overarching problems of today's world—food, births, peace." And one way he tries to tackle these problems is through his relationships with foreign students, who will carry his "gospel" back to their lands after they graduate. He relishes the opportunity to tutor foreign students in English and the sciences, and one of his favorite pastimes is to "get on a blackboard" with a bright young person.

Through his day-to-day activities, this man is striving to pass on what he has learned and thereby help to make his global goals more of a reality.

PROBLEM 6: Tendency to Cast Everyone in the Same Mold

A prominent educator who responded to our survey warned: "The surest way to corrupt the mind of youth is to teach them to hold in higher esteem those who think alike from those who think differently."

This trend toward alikeness in everything was a major concern for a number of our respondents. One achiever creatively referred to this as the "McDonaldization of America— no surprises, no risks, a zero-defect system."

He cautioned that, if we eliminate the people who think differently by teaching them to follow a more standard line, we may lose our most creative individuals—the inventors, artistic innovators, and entrepreneurs our society needs in order to stay on top in the world.

PROBLEM 7: The Specter of War

In a previous study we did, reported in the book *Forecast 2000,* one of the major concerns about the future expressed by those listed in Marquis' *Who's Who In America* was the prospect of war, especially nuclear war. This same fear emerged periodically in this study of success.

For example, one achiever told us America needs to "get off this war binge we now call defense. We can't afford to police the world."

At the same time, our respondents offered few viable solutions. A number of our top achievers are politically active in some way. For example, about 7 in 10 have written to a political official or signed a political petition in the year preceding our survey.

Many seem to sense that political activism and voluntary action may be the most viable roles they can play in dealing with the war and defense issue.

But at least our respondents want to take *some* action. And because of their generally high social, professional, and economic status, when they speak or write about an issue, governmental leaders will probably listen.

PROBLEM 8: Moral Decline

Finally, some top achievers feel the nation is going downhill fast as far as moral and spiritual values are concerned.

161

One executive in a nonprofit organization couched the problem in terms of selfishness:

"A me-first attitude is rampant in our nation today, and it underlies all the other problems we face as a nation. What it all boils down to is simple selfishness.

"Selfishness shows when some discriminate against others, whether from fear or greed. It shows when there's a wide gap between the rich and the poor. It shows when people put their personal, professional goals before the needs of their families.

"Selfishness and ego show when every need and desire must be met immediately, without any evidence of patience or perseverance.

"Selfishness shows up when academic life becomes an apple-polishing, political exercise, without intellectual honesty.

"Selfishness appears in conformity, as those enforcing it are threatened by and squelch those who are different.

"Selfishness shows up in our lack of productivity when people who don't work very hard expect to be well paid.

"And selfishness surfaces as a root cause in our people's past wars, as someone wants something that belongs to someone else."

From every corner, we hear the successful saying there are problems we face now and will continue to face in our society. Yet, on the whole, they're happy and satisfied with their lives.

Thoughtful and critical, they certainly are. But visionary, too. And in most cases, cautiously optimistic.

They are intelligent and perceptive enough to know that, even as they offer criticisms, the same system they're attacking has been very good to them. They've succeeded, often beyond their wildest dreams, in a culture that has defined the rules by which they've played. And, for the most part, they like those rules.

In the main, the successful want to preserve those factors that have been good to them. At the same time, they aspire to correct the more egregious deficiencies—so that those who follow will have a chance to reach even greater heights than they themselves could attain.

CHAPTER

FIELDS OF THE FUTURE

Getting your house in order and reducing the confusion gives you more control over your life. Personal organization somehow releases or frees you to operate more effectively.

Larry King, television and radio talk show host

If you had a crystal ball, discussing the future pattern of your career would all be so simple. But unfortunately, that kind of surefire occupational guidance isn't readily available. Chances are, after leaving college or graduate school or switching from one job to another, you discover the future you planned isn't the Yellow Brick Road you hoped it would be. So you have to take other steps to see where your skills and abilities can best be utilized.

For example, you might want to seek job counseling or career planning. Forty-eight percent of our successful individuals had undergone aptitude testing to help determine their abilities. Also, 33 percent of our total respondents said their tests had revealed an aptitude for their present field. Only 7 percent replied that they hadn't, and 8 percent couldn't recall.

Career planning has become a specialized field with experts to guide you, step by step through every phase of your career. Yet job counselors have to rely heavily on projections, and their advice and recommendations may become largely a matter of conjecture.

So we asked our high-level achievers for career guidance— after all, they know their fields better than anyone and are influential in directing the future of those fields.

First of all, each individual was asked which three fields they would advise young people to consider entering today. Tied for first place, with computers and science, was a piece of good advice rather than a particular occupation. Specifically, about 15 percent gave this answer: "It depends on who the young people are and what really turns them on." Interpretation: you'd do well to have a good grasp of your personal aptitudes and exactly where your interests lie.

Eight clearly identifiable fields also got significant support from our successful individuals. These are their top recommendations:

Computers	15%
Science	15%
Law	10%
Engineering	10%
Medicine	10%
Business	5%
International business	5%
Communications	5%

Other frequently mentioned fields included:

Government	Education
Sociology	Human resources

Publishing   Industrial psychology
History   Construction
Theology   Philosophy
Astronomy   Biochemistry
Biophysics   Adult education
Economics   Administration
     Businesses related
     to the "aging" of
     the population

Now let's move from specific fields to some of the sage advice our respondents offered. For example:

"Be cautious before you commit. The future is mixed." Sound like a Chinese proverb that popped out of a fortune cookie? Actually, it's advice for young people just entering the job market from a successful professor of pediatrics.

And there's more. We asked each high-level achiever in the survey to advise today's youth on how to succeed tomorrow. Here are some of the suggestions offered.

"Be Enthusiastic about Your Field"

People who are the leaders in their fields consider interest and enthusiasm for any chosen field an essential ingredient for success. Almost half of our respondents were very satisfied with their choice of work. And a solid majority of 83 percent said they would choose the same field if they had to start from scratch. Only 8 percent would choose a different field, and 9 percent were uncertain.

Yet a long-time interest in a particular specialty isn't absolutely necessary for success. Only 26 percent of our respondents gave the highest ratings, a 9 or 10, to a long-term interest in their field as an important factor in their success. On the other hand, nearly 4 in 10 gave some degree of importance to this factor (i.e., a rating of 6 or more).

Another indication that a one-career track isn't necessary for super success is the fact that 57 percent had held jobs in other fields.

It is not essential that you stay in one field all your life. Rather, it's more important to have a deep interest and enthusiasm in your line of work, even if you enter it relatively late. You should genuinely *like* what you do; then, if you have sufficient ability, success will be more likely.

One top-notch businessman, an executive vice president for a corporation with more than $1 billion in annual sales, said it this way: "Be enthusiastic about your field. The cream always rises to the top."

This particular executive would definitely do it all over again. With early interests in science and mathematics, he says he always had clear goals for his career. In fact, he is very confident that he has successfully met all the career challenges that have been presented to him.

As an only child, he grew up in a household with an average income, and he got along very well with his family. He learned to read when he was only four and is still an avid reader today.

Before graduating in the top 10 percent of his high school class, he had started his courtship with business by handling a newspaper route. He continued to work part-time through college.

Today, he earns more than $200,000 a year and is actively pursuing other goals—a fact that maintains his interest and enthusiasm at a high level. For example, he hopes to become the president and chairman of the board for a Fortune 500 corporation. For now, he's intent on making his current company a "stronger, more successful corporation."

Now well established in his professional life, this man also participates in the local garden club and various civic organizations. He reads a great deal and enjoys travel and skiing. But he still takes great pleasure in his work.

"Get a Good Education in Your Field and Remain Committed to Learning and Sound Intellectual Principles"

An architect offered this advice to young people as he looked back after many years of work experience. Now almost 80 years old, he finds his career is more administrative than creative, but he still stays active in his field.

This man considers a quality education to have been very instrumental in his rise to the top. Through the years, he's become convinced that "your avocation in life is a continual process of learning more about your field. It can only be achieved when built on a stable foundation of knowledge."

Always an excellent student, our architect graduated valedictorian of his high school class. In college, he discovered his favorite courses related to architecture and engineering, so he completed his graduate studies in architecture.

Now, after years of observation and reflection, he rates his education with an unqualified 10+ in preparing him for his work. But he's still intent on learning more by reading about architecture and history in his spare time.

He sums it up like this: "I would guess from this interview that you will classify me as an educated, happy, conceited old man. You know, you may be right!"

In many ways, this man's attitude and experience parallels that of other successful people we surveyed. As you'll recall, specialized knowledge in a field was one of the highest rated personal success characteristics from our top achievers, with 74 percent scoring themselves an A. In addition, 49 percent responded that they were very satisfied with how their education prepared them for their respective careers.

"Choose Your Graduate School Carefully"

What's in a name? Plenty where success is involved, according to a recent investigation by *U.S. News & World Report*. When in pursuit of higher education, the reputation of the school can be just as important as your track record there.

The magazine suggests that a "name" school carries a lot of weight with job recruiters and personnel managers, especially in the "big leagues" like New York, Chicago, and Los Angeles.

For graduate school, this advice carries double weight, according to a professor we interviewed who works with both undergraduate and graduate students. His research and teaching experience have convinced him that the grad school you choose can make the difference between great success and merely moderate levels of achievement. The important considerations for him seem to be: (1) choose the institution where you feel you'll fit in most naturally and (2) be sure that the one you pick has the best reputation you can find.

This professor, a Ph.D., was awarded partial scholarships for both college and graduate school. He told us that he's very satisfied with the way that his education prepared him for his career. In addition, he continues to educate himself through extensive reading, academic studies, and research.

According to *U.S. News & World Report* (October 3, 1983) MBA graduates are "heavily recruited" from Harvard, Stanford, Wharton, Northwestern, Dartmouth, and the University of Chicago. Law degrees may open even more doors with the "magic names" of Harvard, Yale, Columbia, Stanford, Northwestern, Duke, and Virginia.

To sum up, the key seems to be to find the best possible graduate school that will work for *you* in your field. Then, see if you can get into it.

"Learn to Write and Speak Both Fluently and Effectively"

"I'm fairly fulfilled in my life, having honestly done my best throughout the years—win, lose, or draw," says a prominent professor of medicine. A large part of his success, he says, is due to the fact that he has learned the value of self-expression in doing his best quality work.

Because of the nature of his responsibilities, he has had to draw heavily on his oral and written communication skills. He realized early on that those skills held the power to make or break his career. So, he polished his capabilities in writing and speaking to meet professional standards.

And he's not alone! Of the successful individuals we surveyed, 67 percent graded themselves in the A category for their writing abilities.

Furthermore, 64 percent gave themselves A's for public speaking; and conversational proficiency ranked just behind at 57 percent.

These individuals believe that it's essential to be able to communicate effectively with the public and their peers. So they train themselves to be experts at self-expression.

Another prominent scientist-researcher told us that the scholarly papers he submits for publication have convinced him of the overriding importance of basic writing skills.

"My results almost always have the potential to be published in highly respected professional journals," he explains. "But an inadequate writing ability can put months of research straight into obscurity for lack of a proper presentation. Hard work and important information are invalidated by the lack of translation of an idea to paper; they can easily be lost between head and hand."

This scientist has excelled in his work throughout the years. His research findings are well known on both a national and international level—largely as a result of his ability to communicate. With comfortable earnings and professional achievement, he sees himself as being successful in terms of peer recognition. Now in his late 60s, he says he definitely likes the way his life is going.

Besides professional activities and wide-ranging travel, he enjoys hard physical work, camping, tennis, skiing, and sailing. He belongs to organizations that reflect those interests, such as the Explorers Club, a yacht club, a tennis club, and several professional groups. In all those activities, he finds that his leadership can best be exercised through the writing and speaking skills that he has mastered.

The message of his life seems quite clear: the success-producing impact of good writing and speaking aren't limited to your chosen career. The communications skills you develop on the job will have a ripple effect that can make you more successful in your avocations as well.

"Learn to Be Adaptable and Flexible; Lead Rather than Resist Change"

These words from a laboratory director of military research and development are useful guidelines for dealing with new ideas and innovation on the job.

Because it's easy to get rattled when new ideas are suggested, some people may decide to eliminate all surprise—and beneficial change—from their work. Others may want change for its own sake, thus generating an atmosphere of instability and lack of good judgment.

Our lab director suggests a middle approach. That is, change should not be disruptive and should accommodate the existing situation. With this approach, he's in a position to shift gears more readily for the barrage of innovations that continually rock the scientific community.

172

"It's better to initiate change and lead the pack than to waste energy resisting," he contends.

This researcher is internationally recognized for his work in defense and military products. His career goals, which reflect his advice, are to advance science and technology and to provide better ways of solving the practical problems he encounters in his work.

Beginning with an early interest in science and mathematics, our laboratory director had well-defined goals for his career. Presently, he enjoys the work he does and considers his personal life fairly happy. His spare time is occupied by reading, cabinet making, photography, computer programming, and membership in a professional defense organization. Somewhat ironically, this defense researcher doesn't particularly like the way things are going in this country now, and he rates his satisfaction level at only a 3.

He calls himself an independent in terms of political parties. He claims no belief in a supreme being nor a relationship with God, although he classifies himself a Presbyterian and contributes money to a religious organization.

He doesn't credit luck for his success either. He says his formula for success has been "combined technical and management ability, aggressiveness, dedication, integrity, and hard work."

On the other hand, even though he is a great believer in self-reliance and extensive prior preparation, he remains open to the possibility of surprise. So he advises young people to master adaptability and lead the trends that are changing his field and the world.

Finally, it's interesting to compare this lab director's ideas on innovation and change with the general attitudes of the other successful people we surveyed. When asked to rate how they felt various factors had contributed to their success in their field, 56 percent rated themselves a 9 or 10 for the courage to pursue new ideas or ventures or to take risks. In addition, 44 percent said they are not afraid to be different.

"Learn to Motivate People"

This thought was offered by a certified public accountant, and his experience in this area underscores the advice.

Having managed the office he works in for more than 20 years and having served on the executive board of the firm, he's had plenty of experience leading and influencing people. In fact, he gives himself an A for that personal skill. Similarly, in their self-appraisals of personal skills, 56 percent of other high achievers awarded an A grade to their ability to motivate subordinates.

This CPA has helped his firm grow to a position of major influence in his community. Now, facing retirement, he plans to keep promoting the company and to spend more time in volunteer service.

Moreover, his career has been a prosperous one—he earns more than $200,000 a year. He recalls the two people who influenced him and motivated him toward success: a neighborhood grocer and an older college student.

His life today is on the whole very satisfying; on a scale of zero to 10, he awarded a score of 9 to his feelings of satisfaction with his family relationships. And he says his personal life in general is very happy. A religious man, he believes that God has a plan for his life, and he considers his relationship with God a very close and personal one.

Finally, it seems that the advice and inspiration this accountant received as a young man was an important ingredient that taught him how to motivate others later. And clearly, the advice he offers is rooted in his own career experience and personal success.

"Don't Always Expect Material Gain to Accompany Personal Satisfaction"

Those words come from a pediatrician who definitely practices what he preaches. Active now in teaching and administration in public health, this doctor is more concerned with the human condition than in acquiring material wealth.

Although he considers money and material belongings a common reward of success, he doesn't own any luxury items. In fact, he says the desire to make money in his field wasn't a factor in his success, and he rates the money motive a zero.

Still busy teaching, lecturing, and consulting in his field, he would like to be remembered as an innovator. He is currently working on an international level as a consultant to promote better conditions for Latin American medical students.

Does his work make him happy on a personal basis? Yes, he says, very happy, except for occasional depression he experiences from a feeling that he may have "failed to capitalize on my full potential."

He highly recommends that young people seek self-fulfillment ahead of material gain. His personal formula for success reflects this advice: "Success results from a sense of personal service combined with scientific and academic integrity, always with the goal of excellence."

"Go for It—and Believe You Can Do It"

All of the successful individuals we questioned have one thing in common—each of them tried for the top. They had the highest of aspirations and a positive, can-do attitude.

Six out of 10 awarded themselves A's in self-confidence when asked to rate their perceived skills and weaknesses.

A southwestern entrepreneur we interviewed gave himself an A— in self-confidence. And he advises young people, "Go for it! Believe you can, and you *will!*"

With an annual income of more than $200,000, he has many of the material privileges of success. Predictably, he rates his satisfaction with his standard of living a perfect 10.

His favorite activities are far ranging, and some, though not all, require money: boating, fishing, hunting, playing the piano, reading, and conversation with friends.

Although this man is an example of the supreme positive thinker, he's not obsessed by ambition, rating his ambition and desire to get ahead in his field an 8. He also gives an 8 to his level of satisfaction in his work.

Also, even though he always thought he could succeed, he *didn't* always have clear goals for his career. In fact, he held several other jobs before he settled down to his present position. But when the opportunity to start his business came along, he did go for it. And he *achieved* it.

And how does he know that he's reached the top?

He says the main criteria are "position and peer recognition." Now in his early 50s, he also has further goals. He'd like to build his firm to a position of greater leadership in his field, and he'd like to pursue high-level government service.

So despite his past achievements, this businessman still believes he can go further up the ladder of success. In fact, he rates his achievements an 8 out of 10—not quite at the top. But he rates the sense of personal worth that he has achieved at 9.

But even as we share this advice from the nation's most successful people, it's necessary to offer a word of caution. The thoughts and principles are merely reflections of an underlying attitude that says, "I understand myself, my strengths and weaknesses. I think I have the potential to develop and improve. And I believe there's a way to marshal my personal assets, now and in the future, to maximize my chances for success in life."

The starting point to achieve all that's within your capabilities is to believe in yourself. It's Peale's power of positive thinking and Schuller's possibility thinking rolled into one.

Once you've decided you *can* and *will* accomplish your goals, success becomes more a dynamic style of life than an ultimate state of being. It's the ongoing process of developing certain key traits and tricks of the trade that pave the way to peaks of achievement.

Before you try to take the first step to a successful future, it's important to know where you stand right now. What are your present strengths and weaknesses that may help or hinder you as you try to achieve your maximum career potential? To answer this question, let's turn to a consideration of your success quotient.

CHAPTER

WHAT'S YOUR SUCCESS QUOTIENT?

A formula for success: "First and foremost, being funny. Then, not necessarily in order: uniqueness; ability to rivet an audience's attention on what you're doing; ability to control an audience; ability to think quickly on your feet; ability to have the audience like you; ability to discard what isn't funny and hold onto what is funny."

Don Rickles, comedian

Now that we've covered all the highlights of what it takes to be a success, how do you measure up? Do you have what it takes to succeed in a big way? Or are there still some areas in your personal and career life that need more work?

To help you determine where you stand on the road to high achievement, we've devised a special test. This Success Quotient test, as we call it, is based on the questionnaire we circulated among those listed in Marquis' *Who's Who In America*. Unlike an Intelligence Quotient, or IQ, however, this number is under your control: It can rise significantly during adulthood as you work to develop certain success-oriented skills. So look on your Success Quotient not as a static determination of your potential to achieve but simply as an indicator of what you should do to improve your possibilities in life.

Two caveats are in order, however. As we mentioned in the preface, there are always exceptions to any formula for success. There are "mavericks" who somehow don't fit into any mold. They seem to break all the rules, yet they manage to rise to the top. Also, most success stories have a mysterious extra ingredient, a kind of "X factor," which can't be quantified in any sort of objective test.

Still, your Success Quotient should give you some solid indications about how closely your qualities, skills, and background parallel those who have reached the top in various fields.

Now, for a few mundane instructions on good testmanship: Don't ponder any of the questions too long; after you've reflected for a moment or two, just give the response that seems most accurate and move on to the next topic. Don't consult the appendix, which contains the responses of the high achievers we interviewed. Looking at those results could influence your answers.

Finally, and most important, *be honest with yourself.* Don't indicate the qualities, traits, skills, or background you *wish* you had, but rather, those you genuinely feel you *do* have, right now.

When you reach the end, we'll provide a scale to help you see where you stand in the broad sweep of Great American Success Stories.

THE GREAT AMERICAN SUCCESS QUOTIENT TEST

1. Listed below under general headings are FACTORS that are often mentioned as CONTRIBUTING to success in one's chosen field. Indicate how important you feel each factor has been *in your own case* by rating it on a scale

from zero to 10—the higher the number the more important, and the lower the number the less important.

A. Personal Characteristics or Traits

a.	Intelligence	0 1 2 3 4 5 6 7 8 9 10
b.	Common sense	0 1 2 3 4 5 6 7 8 9 10
c.	Special talent in specific area	0 1 2 3 4 5 6 7 8 9 10
d.	Having a broad range of interests	0 1 2 3 4 5 6 7 8 9 10
e.	Not being afraid to be different	0 1 2 3 4 5 6 7 8 9 10
f.	Tolerance of other viewpoints	0 1 2 3 4 5 6 7 8 9 10
g.	Caring about other people	0 1 2 3 4 5 6 7 8 9 10
h.	Being a hard worker	0 1 2 3 4 5 6 7 8 9 10
i.	Not being afraid to pursue new ideas, ventures, take risks	0 1 2 3 4 5 6 7 8 9 10
j.	Establishing well-defined personal goals	0 1 2 3 4 5 6 7 8 9 10
k.	Ambition, desire to get ahead	0 1 2 3 4 5 6 7 8 9 10

B. Family Environment and Influence

a.	Physical environment or habitat when young	0 1 2 3 4 5 6 7 8 9 10
b.	National ancestry, parent's ancestors, nationality	0 1 2 3 4 5 6 7 8 9 10

181

c.	Material advantages, money, property	0 1 2 3 4 5 6 7 8 9 10
d.	Strong support of parents	0 1 2 3 4 5 6 7 8 9 10
e.	Happiness of home life	0 1 2 3 4 5 6 7 8 9 10
f.	Strong support of other family members	0 1 2 3 4 5 6 7 8 9 10
g.	Strong religious upbringing	0 1 2 3 4 5 6 7 8 9 10
h.	Important personal contacts	0 1 2 3 4 5 6 7 8 9 10

C. Academic Experience

a.	Getting good grades	0 1 2 3 4 5 6 7 8 9 10
b.	Scoring well on achievement tests	0 1 2 3 4 5 6 7 8 9 10
c.	Working hard at school work	0 1 2 3 4 5 6 7 8 9 10
d.	Having natural learning ability	0 1 2 3 4 5 6 7 8 9 10
e.	Good work habits, ability to organize time, get things done	0 1 2 3 4 5 6 7 8 9 10
f.	Influence and encouragement of teachers	0 1 2 3 4 5 6 7 8 9 10
g.	Involvement in sports	0 1 2 3 4 5 6 7 8 9 10
h.	Desire to excel	0 1 2 3 4 5 6 7 8 9 10
i.	Having specific academic goals	0 1 2 3 4 5 6 7 8 9 10
j.	Involvement in extracurricular activities	0 1 2 3 4 5 6 7 8 9 10
k.	Attending high-quality school(s)	0 1 2 3 4 5 6 7 8 9 10

D. Outside (School) Interests

a. Having a broad range of   0 1 2 3 4 5 6 7 8 9 10
   interests (outside school)
b. Having outside jobs, sum-   0 1 2 3 4 5 6 7 8 9 10
   mer work, etc.

E. Experiences in Chosen Field

a. Ambition, desire to get   0 1 2 3 4 5 6 7 8 9 10
   ahead
b. Special talent in chosen   0 1 2 3 4 5 6 7 8 9 10
   field
c. A boss, superiors who as-   0 1 2 3 4 5 6 7 8 9 10
   sisted or advised
d. Supportive co-workers   0 1 2 3 4 5 6 7 8 9 10
e. Hard work, diligence   0 1 2 3 4 5 6 7 8 9 10
f. Luck, timing, being at the 0 1 2 3 4 5 6 7 8 9 10
   right place at the right
   time
g. Choosing right field at   0 1 2 3 4 5 6 7 8 9 10
   right time
h. Having long-time interest   0 1 2 3 4 5 6 7 8 9 10
   in the field
i. Desire to make money   0 1 2 3 4 5 6 7 8 9 10
j. Organizational ability   0 1 2 3 4 5 6 7 8 9 10
k. Ability to follow instruc- 0 1 2 3 4 5 6 7 8 9 10
   tions
l. Ability to motivate subor- 0 1 2 3 4 5 6 7 8 9 10
   dinates
m. Respect for peers   0 1 2 3 4 5 6 7 8 9 10
n. Ability to get things done 0 1 2 3 4 5 6 7 8 9 10

2. Have you always had pretty clear goals for your life?
___ Yes ___ No

3. Do you feel you have achieved your goals in life, or are there further goals you would like to achieve?
___ Achieved goals ___ Further goals

4. Have you always had pretty clear goals for your *career?*
___ Yes ___ No

5. How happy a childhood did you have?
___ Very happy ___ Fairly happy ___ Fairly unhappy ___ Very unhappy

6. How well did you get along with your father?
___ Very well ___ Fairly well ___ Not too well ___ Not at all

7. How well did you get along with your mother?
___ Very well ___ Fairly well ___ Not too well ___ Not at all

8. Outside of school, how much reading did you do in your early years—that is, before the age of 10—compared to other children that age?
___ Much more ___ Somewhat more ___ About the same ___ Somewhat less ___ Much less

9. Outside of school, how much reading did you do during *your high school years* compared to other students that age?
___ Much more ___ Somewhat more ___ About the same ___ Somewhat less ___ Much less

10. Outside of your required school reading, how much reading did you do during your college years compared to other students that age?

___ Much more ___ Somewhat more ___ About the same ___ Somewhat less ___ Much less

11. What was your standing in your senior year in high school? That is, what percentile were you in (e.g., the top 10th, bottom quarter, etc.)? _____

12. What was your class standing in your senior year of college? _____

13. If you've taken an IQ test, what was your score? _____ (score)

14. Were your grades about the same for all of your courses or were they higher in some courses than in others?

___ All about the same ___ Better in some courses

15. How important was it to your parents that you got good grades?

___ Very important ___ Fairly important ___ Not very important ___ Not at all important

16. Did you ever have a teacher or teachers who made you enthusiastic about a particular subject?

___ Yes ___ No

17. Were you an officer of your class, of any school organization, or a team captain of any athletic team in high school?

___ Yes ___ No

18. Were you an officer of your class, of any school organization, or a team captain of any athletic team in college?

___ Yes ___ No

19. Did you have any part-time or full-time jobs when you were in high school?

___ Yes ___ No

20. Did you have any part-time or full-time jobs when you were in college?

____ Yes   ____ No

Self Appraisal

21. Looking at myself as objectively as I can (or as some other person would), I would give myself the following grade for each of the following areas. (CHECK GRADE)

	A+	A	A−	B+	B	B−	C+	C	C−	D	Fail
a. Ability to get along with others											
b. Ability to make money											
c. Self-confidence											
d. Self-reliance											
e. Conversational ability											
f. Writing skill											
g. Reading skill											
h. Public speaking ability											
i. Willpower											
j. Ability to get things done											
k. Ability to motivate subordinates											
l. Ability to put orders from superiors into effect											
m. General intelligence											
n. Common sense											
o. Specialized knowledge required in your field											
p. Intuition											
q. Creativity, inventiveness											
r. Work habits											
s. Organizational ability											
t. Leadership ability											

Personal Characteristics

22. Indicate how accurately the following statements describe you personally—the higher the number you select,

the more you feel that statement describes you—the lower the number, the less accurately it describes you.

	0	1	2	3	4	5	6	7	8	9	10
a. I was just born lucky.											
b. I have a broad range of interests.											
c. I am not afraid to be different.											
d. I am tolerant of other viewpoints.											
e. I care a great deal about other people.											
f. I am not afraid to take chances or risks.											
g. I have well-defined personal goals.											
h. I believe in a supreme being.											
i. I believe that God has a plan for my life.											
j. I feel I have a close personal relationship with God.											
k. I have a strong sense of right and wrong.											

23. About how many books have you read during the last 12 months?

    ___ Fiction   ___ Nonfiction

24. On a typical day, how many hours do you spend watching television?

    ___ Hours

25. About how many hours per week do you spend in volunteer activities?

    ___ Hours per week

26. Which, if any, of these have you done in the past 12 months?

    ___ Donated money to a charitable cause
    ___ Given money to a religious organization
    ___ Donated time to helping poor, disadvantaged, or needy people

187

___ Donated time to religious work
___ Written a letter to a political official or signed a political petition
___ None of these

27. What was the last grade you completed in school? _____

28. What is your age? _____

This concludes the test to help you determine your Success Quotient. Now, let's turn to an evaluation of your answers.

EVALUATION OF YOUR SUCCESS QUOTIENT TEST

Award yourself the following points, depending on your answer to each question:

Question:

1—**Section A:** For each of subsections *b, h,* and *i,* give yourself 6 points if you scored 9 or 10; 5 points if you scored 7 or 8; and 2 points if you scored 5 or 6.

For each of subsections *g, e, a,* and *k,* give yourself 5 points if you scored 9 or 10; 4 points if you scored 7 or 8; and 1 point if you scored 5 or 6.

For each of subsections *f, d, j,* and *c,* give yourself 4 points if you scored 9 or 10; 3 points if you scored 7 or 8; and 1 point if you scored 5 or 6.

1—**Section B:** For each of subsections *a, e, d,* and *f,* give yourself 4 points if you scored 9 or 10; 3 points if you scored 7 or 8; and 1 point if you scored 5 or 6.

For each of subsections *g, b,* and *h,* give yourself 3 points if you scored 9 or 10 and 2 points if you scored 7 or 8.

For subsection *c,* give yourself 1 point if you scored between 7 and 10.

1—Section C: For each of subsections *h* and *e*, give yourself 6 points if you scored 9 or 10; 5 points if you scored 7 or 8; and 2 points if you scored 5 or 6.

For each of subsections *d* and *c*, give yourself 5 points if you scored 9 or 10; 4 points if you scored 7 or 8; and 1 point if you scored 5 or 6.

For each of subsections *k*, *a*, *f*, *b*, and *i*, give yourself 4 points if you scored 9 or 10; 3 points if you scored 7 or 8; and 1 point if you scored 5 or 6.

For each of subsections *j* and *g*, give yourself 3 points if you scored 9 or 10 and 2 points if you scored 7 or 8.

1—Section D: For each of subsections *a* and *b*, give yourself 3 points if you scored 9 or 10 and 2 points if you scored 7 or 8.

1—Section E: For each of subsections *n* and *e*, give yourself 6 points if you scored 9 or 10; 5 points if you scored 7 or 8; and 2 points if you scored 5 or 6.

For each of subsections *a* and *l*, give yourself 5 points if you scored 9 or 10; 4 points if you scored 7 or 8; and 1 point if you scored 5 or 6.

For each of subsections *f*, *m*, *j*, *b*, *k*, *c*, *g*, *h*, *d*, and *i*, give yourself 3 points if you scored 9 or 10 and 2 points if you scored 6 to 8.

2. Give yourself 6 points if you answered yes.

3. Give yourself 6 points if you answered Further goals.

4. Give yourself 6 points if you answered yes.

5. Give yourself 3 points if you answered Very happy and 2 points if you answered Fairly happy.

6. Give yourself 3 points if you answered Very well and 2 points if you answered Fairly well.

7. Give yourself 4 points if you answered Very well and 2 points if you answered Fairly well.

8. Give yourself 6 points if you answered Much more, 4 points if you answered Somewhat more, and 1 point if you answered About the same.

9. Give yourself 6 points if you answered Much more, 4

points if you answered Somewhat more, and 1 point if you answered About the same.

10. Give yourself 5 points if you answered Much more, 4 points if you answered Somewhat more, and 1 point if you answered About the same.

11. Give yourself 8 points if you were first in your class; 7 points if you were from 2d to 5th in the class; 6 points if you were in the top 10th; and 2 points if you were in the top quarter to top 10th.

12. Give yourself 8 points if you were first in the class; 7 points if you were from 2d to 5th in the class; 6 points if you were in the top 10th; and 2 points if you were in the top quarter to top 10th.

13. Give yourself 5 points if your IQ is 130 to 139; 6 points if it's 140 to 149; and 7 points if it's 150 or above.

14. Give yourself 4 points if you answered Better in some courses.

15. Give yourself 4 points if you answered Very important and 3 points if you answered Fairly important.

16. Give yourself 5 points if you answered yes.

17. Give yourself 3 points if you answered yes.

18. Give yourself 3 points if you answered yes.

19. Give yourself 5 points if you answered yes.

20. Give yourself 5 points if you answered yes.

21. For each of subsections n, o, d, m, and j, give yourself 8 points if you scored in the A range and 4 points if you scored in the B range.

For each of subsections a, t, q, g, f, p, s, h, c, l, r, k, e, and i, give yourself 6 points if you scored in the A range and 3 points if you scored in the B range.

For subsection b, give yourself 4 points if you scored in the A range and 3 points if you scored in the B range.

22. For subsection k, give yourself 6 points if you scored 9 or 10; 5 points if you scored 7 or 8; and 2 points if you scored 5 or 6.

For each of subsections *h, c, d, e, b, f,* and *g,* give yourself 5 points if you scored 9 or 10; 4 points if you scored 7 or 8; and 1 point if you scored 5 or 6.

For each of subsections *j, i,* and *a,* give yourself 3 points if you scored 9 or 10 and 2 points if you scored 7 or 8.

23. Give yourself 6 points if you read more than 26 books; 5 points if you read 16 to 25 books; and 4 points if you read 11 to 15.

24. Give yourself 4 points if you watch 1.4 hours of television or less per day.

25. Give yourself 3 points if you spend more than 3 hours a week.

26. Give yourself 1 point for each of the activities or donations you engaged in. If you answered None of these, subtract 1 point.

27. Give yourself 8 points if you earned a graduate degree after college; 5 points if you attended graduate school after college without graduating; and 4 points if you graduated from college without attending graduate school.

28. Give yourself 13 points if you're 29 years old or younger; 10 points if you're 30 to 39; 7 points if you're 40 to 49; and 4 points if you're 50 to 59.

Now, for the moment of truth: What's your Success Quotient—and what does it mean for your potential to achieve great things?

You can figure your Success Quotient (SQ) quite easily. Just follow this simple, three-step procedure:

1. Add up all the points you were awarded in the above test. This is your raw success score.
2. Divide this raw score by 5.
3. Round off the result to the nearest whole number.

Here's a sample calculation. Suppose your raw point score adds up to 301. You divide this figure by 5 to get 60.2. Then you round off to get 60, which is your Success Quotient, or SQ.

But what does it mean? We interpret the SQ score this way:

- An SQ of less than 30 means your chances to succeed at this point are *poor*. Of course, this doesn't mean you can't improve. On the contrary, you can! That's one of the basic messages of this book. But you should at least be aware that you have some work to do if you hope to have a good chance to succeed.
- As SQ of 30 to 49 means you have only a *fair* chance for success. But again, you can improve your possibilities with effort.
- If you scored 50 to 69, your chances of succeeding are *good,* but it's essential that you continue developing in those areas where you're weak.
- If you scored 70 to 79, your chances for success are *excellent.* Just keep up the good work and fine-tune your few rough spots.
- An SQ of 80 to 89 means you're practically a *sure bet* for success.
- If you rolled up 90 points or more, you should be a big success already!

And now, a few words of explanation: First, as we've seen throughout this book, success can be an elusive concept. What is great achievement for one person may be a rather ho-hum accomplishment for another.

Also, there's that tough distinction between the inner sense of achievement and the traditional outward manifestations. In other words, one person may *feel* highly successful even though he's accomplished much less than another. In short, your chance to experience success depends as much on your understanding of what success is as it does on your Success Quotient.

There are also other problems with devising a test like this. Obviously, different skills are required to succeed in different fields, but unfortunately, it's impossible to test them all in a general evaluation of this type.

We face many limitations when we try to devise one Success Quotient for those in every field of endeavor. Even as we talk about identifying your Success Quotient, we understand that there are many factors and considerations that can't be captured by one short test and a sum of points.

On the other hand, there are some solid reasons to consider your score as an indicator, however rough, of your chances to succeed. The questions you've answered are exactly the same as the ones we've asked the most successful people in the United States. And the points we've assigned to each answer are weighted according to the responses we received from these top achievers.

CHAPTER

THE PEAK OF THE MOUNTAIN

Nothing is impossible. When someone tells me something can't be done, that's a challenge for me to do it.

U.S. Senator Paula Hawkins

As we've examined the meaning of success, we've done our best to answer basic questions about what success is and how you can achieve it. If it seems impossible to wrap the whole subject into one neat package, that's probably just as well, since there are as many definitions and experiences of success as there are successful people.

One of the advantages of taking surveys to determine the backgrounds, traits, attitudes, and lifestyles of successful people is that this gives us a helpful overview of what success is. Also, when we understand what most successful people are like—how they feel and what actions they've taken in the past to get where they are now—we have definite standards to keep in mind and clear-cut targets to shoot for.

But broad surveys also have a disadvantage because they can cause us to focus on what most people have done, instead of what *I, individually* should do to reach the top. That's one of the reasons we've included so many individual case studies in this book—to convey the wide variety of experiences that are possible. Our study shows that there's no one path to the peak of the mountain.

Now, let's spend a few final moments considering how you, personally, can benefit most from some of the ingredients of the success stories we've studied. We like to think of these ingredients in terms of attitudes, rather than hard-and-fast rules or principles. After all, the success evidenced in outward trappings—material possessions, social status, or peer recognition—arises from an inner state. It's wrapped up in personal drive and in the belief that a certain level of achievement is possible.

Let's focus on those inner attitudes that are most likely to provide the foundation for a successful life.

ATTITUDE 1: Regard Material Rewards as a By-Product Not a Goal of Success

The successful people we surveyed had high incomes and material possessions, but they didn't make those things the be-all and end-all of their lives.

ATTITUDE 2: Don't Plan to Rest on Your Laurels

The top achievers we studied believe society needs to be changed, and they're acting to effect those reforms. In a sense, they're programmed to keep contributing. They never make the assumption that they've arrived. Personality traits they've developed throughout their lives prompt them to keep driving forward.

ATTITUDE 3: Success Isn't Necessarily a Matter of Genius

Our Marquis' *Who's Who* group certainly did well on their IQ tests. But they place a greater importance on other personal factors, such as the ability to get things done, the desire to achieve, and an ability to organize. You don't have to be a genius to be a success.

ATTITUDE 4: Place a High Premium on Developing Common Sense

The ability to exercise good, practical judgments in the everyday affairs of life appears to be more important than raw intelligence.

ATTITUDE 5: Religious Commitment May or May Not Play a Role in Worldly Achievement

As we've seen, two out of five of our top achievers weren't particularly religious. Faith, it seems, isn't essential for success. But if a person's belief system is heartfelt and mature, faith may provide inner strengths that can enhance the possibility of success.

ATTITUDE 6: Don't Expect Success to Fall into Your Lap

Those we interviewed indicated there's no substitute for hard work, long hours, organization, and getting things done.

Few place a high premium on the advantages of being born into a wealthy or prominent family or other factors outside their control.

ATTITUDE 7: Develop a Clear Set of Goals

Most top achievers have had clear goals for their lives and careers.

ATTITUDE 8: Don't Allow Yourself to Get Discouraged by Obstacles to Success in Your Life

Some of the achievers we surveyed cited the ability to overcome adverse conditions as a reason for their success. They had something to fight against—the Depression, an unhappy childhood, or discrimination.

ATTITUDE 9: Look for a Special Person to Put You on the Fast Track to the Top

Many people mentioned individuals other than their parents who had a special influence on their life goals (e.g., a teacher, a coach, or a friend). Even adults may be open to guidance by such a person. This attitude is especially important when dealing with your own children or other young people: reach out and give them some encouragement!

ATTITUDE 10: Fall in Love with Books

Practically all the successful people we contacted have always been heavy readers—beginning in grade school and continuing through high school, college, and their adult lives.

ATTITUDE 11: Part-Time Work Is an Important Experience for Young People

Again, this is an important message for parents. Work outside school teaches youngsters to be self-sufficient, independent, and responsible.

ATTITUDE 12: You Can Be a Success in More Than One Field

This is an especially important point because many young people think they have to find the one right occupation. In fact, many of those in our survey thought they could have been a success in other fields. And a number *are* successes in more than one line of work. In short, a success is a success is a success—the main ingredient is not the particular field but the development of inner traits and attitudes.

ATTITUDE 13: Don't Expect High Achievement to Bring Supreme Happiness

Success is not the Holy Grail—at least not for most people. Top achievers tend to be happier than the general public, probably because they've found a field they really enjoy. Unlike the general public, most say they would go into the same line of work if they had to do it over again.

But still, only about half the achievers we studied listed themselves as very happy or extremely satisfied with all aspects of their lives. One obvious conclusion is that many successful people have the same problems as everyone else. High achievement is only one of many factors that can help bring true happiness and contentment.

ATTITUDE 14: As You Become More Successful, Begin to Share Your Success with Others

Those we surveyed tend to be a caring, giving, concerned segment of society. And they're interested in and committed to shaping the future with their gifts and volunteer activities. This open-ended approach to sharing their success seems to play a role in their achievement of high position. As they give to others, their gifts are returned to them manyfold.

With such attitudes, the striving for success becomes an experience of inner growth, rather than just an effort to push, shove, and scramble one's way to the top. Drive, ambition, intensity, and singleness of purpose are certainly valuable qualities for the person who wants to succeed. But perhaps the key lesson in the Great American Success Story is that achievement should never be an end in itself.

The idea is not just to work to finish a task but rather to work well and to savor each step you take up the mountain you've chosen. Then, when you reach the top, you won't feel spent from all the effort. In fact, you won't even feel you've arrived. Instead, you'll feel refreshed and invigorated by what you've accomplished, and you'll find yourself looking for the next peak to conquer.

Appendix

SUCCESS SURVEY FINDINGS

APPENDIX

LEVEL OF SUCCESS ACHIEVED AS THE NATION'S MOST SUCCESSFUL PEOPLE PERCEIVE IT

A large majority of the nation's top achievers apparently agree with their designation in Who's Who as the most successful Americans. When the sample of persons listed in Who's Who is asked to indicate to what degree they feel they have achieved success on an 11-point scale (with 10 representing total success and 0 no success), 83 percent grade themselves at least an 8. At the same time, however, only 13 percent say they have attained--the pinnacle of success--a perfect 10 on the success scale.

These top achievers apparently also believe they would have been a success no matter what field they were in. Eight in 10 stated they would have been as successful in another occupation as they were in the one they chose.

THE "FORMULA FOR SUCCESS" ACCORDING TO THE NATION'S HIGH ACHIEVERS

When the nation's top achievers are asked to rate the factors they consider most important in contributing to their own success, hard work emerges as the highest-rated factor, with about 7 in 10 grading it 9 or 10. This applies not only to respondents' precareer training, but also to their present occupations.

Ambition and the desire to excel are rated next most important, with about half the respondents giving these factors a very important (9 or 10) rating.

Intelligence, getting good grades in school, scoring well on achievement tests, and natural learning ability are rated surprisingly low.

Rated next lowest in importance are various attributes associated with social or management skills, such as the ability to motivate subordinates, respecting one's peers, and tolerating other viewpoints.

Relatively few of the high achievers credit religion as an important factor in their success. Only 16 percent, for example, feel that a strong religious upbringing contributed to their success in life. And they appear not to be particularly religious—at least in a formal sense. Only about one in five believes that he or she has a close personal relationship with God or that God has a plan for his or her life. Similarly, only about 6 in 10 believe in a supreme being—far below the 95% figure for the American public.

Rated least important by high achievers are circumstances pertaining to family environment including happiness of home life, strong support of family members, and personal contacts, followed by such factors as involvement in sports and extracurricular activities at school, and—least of all—the desire for material possessions and money.

While the three basic occupational groups comprising the sample of achievers—educators, professionals other than educators, and businesspeople—agree that the key factors in success are hard work and ambition, some differences emerge as to the relative importance of *other* factors, depending on respondents' field of endeavor.

Businesspeople, for example, place much more value on ambition or the desire to get ahead and on such talents as organizational ability and the ability to motivate others. And they give greater weight to the desire to make money than do either professionals or educators.

In contrast, educators place much higher priorities on getting good grades, scoring well on achievement tests, native intelligence, learning ability, and attending the right college.

BACKGROUND FOR SUCCESS

In addition to analyzing respondents testimony concerning what they feel are the essential elements that contributed to their success, it is also important to examine their backgrounds, beginning with childhood and family influences through schooling and work experiences, to identify the factors that help determine high achievement. Many of the survey findings point to differences in background between high achievers and their less illustrious contemporaries.

One important way in which America's top achievers differ from average citizens is that roughly two in three established specific goals for both their lives and their careers at an early stage in life.

A large proportion of the top achievers held leadership roles in high school and college even though they may not have been more popular than other students. For example, about 6 in 10 of the high achievers were either class officers or team captains in high school, and almost as high a proportion (5 in 10) held such positions in college, although they had about the same number of friends in school as did their peers.

One significant activity that distinguishes high achievers from their less successful counterparts is their love of reading—and their corresponding lack of interest in television.

This interest in reading (aside from assigned school work) began in elementary school, continued through high school and college, and is still evident today.

About three-fourths of those sampled say they read more than their contemporaries during their elementary and high school years. Also, almost 6 in 10 stated they read more than their college classmates.

Today, these high achievers read an average of almost 20 books during the last year, roughly divided between fiction and nonfiction, far higher than the average number of books read by the American public.

Not surprisingly, educators read an average of 25 books during the last 12 months. But even those in other professions and in business averaged as many as 15 and 12 books, respectively, during the same period.

Compared to the American public, who spend an average of three to four hours each day watching TV, the top achievers are in front of their television sets for only about an hour and a half.

The perceptions of the top achievers regarding the factors contributing to their success frequently differ from actuality when their backgrounds are examined.

Although the top achievers assign relatively little importance to their family background as contributing to their success, a disproportionately high percentage of their parents were better educated than their contemporaries.

For example, almost half of the fathers of the top achievers had a college education or better, and one third of their mothers attended college.

These figures are well above the national norms, considering that, given the relatively advanced ages of the achievers sample, the parents would have been educated during the 1920s and 30s.

Although relatively few of these successful people admit to being born into a privileged family economic situation, the fact remains that, given the high educational attainment of their parents, they were brought up in higher-than-average-income homes.

One of the most significant differences between achievers and average Americans are the achievers' class standing in both high school and college. But again, achievers tend to play down both of these factors in their success.

Two thirds of the sample were in the top 10 of their class in high school, and half were in the top 10 of their college class.

Despite the fact that top achievers award relatively little importance to native intelligence as a factor in success, a large majority rated their own intelligence as either A+, A, or A−. (Reinforcing this self-perception of intelligence, one quarter of *the achievers reported an IQ of 130 or over even though 60 percent either had not taken such a test or could not remember their score.*)

However, the successful grade themselves differently depending on their field of endeavor. Educators, followed by other professionals, assign themselves somewhat higher grades for intelligence and communication skills (speaking, writing, etc.) than do their counterparts in the world of business.

In contrast, those in business grade themselves higher than either educators or other professionals in leadership ability, the ability to carry out orders from their superiors, the ability to motivate subordinates—and, not surprisingly, the ability to make money.

The nation's top achievers are somewhat more likely to have been involved in athletics and extracurricular activities in both high school and college than average Americans. Again, however, high achievers tend to rate these activities as not contributing significantly to their success.

Half the sample was involved in athletics in high school, and 3 in 10 participated while in college. Similarly, 8 in 10 participated in extracurricular activities in their high school years, and as many as 7 in 10 did so in college.

THE REWARDS OF SUCCESS AS PERCEIVED BY HIGH ACHIEVERS

When America's achievers are asked to indicate what they feel are the rewards of success, the majority respond in personal rather than material terms, with self-fulfillment emerging as by far the most important reward. Eight in 10 for example give a "sense of personal worth" or "self-respect" the highest score of 9 or 10.

The most frequently cited rewards (cited by approximately 6 in 10) are "recognition by one's peers" and "being able to contribute to society".

Of relatively little importance in the eyes of the achievers is public recognition. And of almost no admitted consequence are the material rewards of success; e.g., affluence, expensive belongings, and such related advantages as personal power and social status. Less than 1 person in 10, for example, rated any of these factors as very important.

At the same time, however, it is interesting to note that most of the nation's top achievers have acquired the material rewards and trappings of success. Four in 10 have incomes of $100,000 a year or more, as many as 3 in 10 own two or more homes, and 1 in 6 has a swimming pool

Differences also are found in the perceived importance of the rewards of success, depending on occupation. People in business, for example, are about twice as likely as educators to feel that material rewards, money, and personal power are very important. Similarly, social status is more likely to be considered very important by businesspeople than by those in education. Persons in professions other than education fall somewhere between educators and those in business regarding the importance of these factors.

A key question, of course, is if success has brought happiness and satisfaction to the lives of the top achievers. Evidence from the survey strongly suggests that it has when compared with the findings for the American population as a whole.

At least ostensibly, the nation's top achievers are happier than ordinary Americans. They are more satisfied with their lives overall and with key aspects of their lives, such as their standards of living and their jobs. Reinforcing this evidence of job satisfaction is the fact that more than 8 in 10 of the high-achieving sample said they would go into the same field or line of work if starting over again.

THE CONTRIBUTIONS OF
HIGH ACHIEVERS

The survey reveals that the nation's high achievers are not content to rest on their laurels but have used their lofty station to contribute to society and to help those less fortunate.

As a group they are altruistic to a remarkable degree. Six in 10 are involved in volunteer activities, and they spend an average of three hours a week in these efforts.

Virtually the entire sample donated money to various causes within the last year, and, despite the fact that the high achievers are not religious in the formal sense, almost 7 in 10 gave money to religious organizations. These proportions are even higher among the business and professional groups in the survey.

The top achievers are also heavily involved in the political process. As many as 7 in 10 have either written to a public official or signed a petition within the last year.

PERCEIVED DEGREE OF SUCCESS IN ONE'S FIELD

To what degree do you feel that you have been a success in your line of work? To indicate this would you circle a number between zero and ten—the higher the number, the more successful you feel you have been, the lower the number the less successful.

		OCCUPATION			INCOME			
	TOTAL	Educa-tion	Other Profes-sional	Busi-ness	$200K & Over	$100K-199K	$50K-99K	Under $50K
	%	%	%	%	%	%	%	%
10	13	11	16	15	17	15	9	13
9	30	29	36	31	37	30	32	19
8	40	44	33	40	33	41	42	40
7	9	8	8	8	6	9	10	12
6	2	2	2	1	*	1	2	7
5	1	1	1	1	1	1	1	2
Under 5	2	1	1	3	2	2	1	1
Undesignated	3	4	3	1	4	1	3	6
	100%	100%	100%	100%	100%	100%	100%	100%

PERCEIVED REWARDS OF SUCCESS

RELATIVE IMPORTANCE OF VARIOUS "REWARDS"

Listed below are some of the factors that are frequently mentioned as being the REWARDS of success in one's field of endeavor. To indicate how important you feel each of these is, would you rate it from zero to ten—zero if you feel it is of no importance and ten if you feel it is of the highest importance.

IMPORTANCE RATING

	Very Important (9-10)	Fairly Important (6 8)	Neither Important nor Unimportant (5)	Fairly Unimportant (2-4)	Very Unimportant (0-1)	No Opinion
	%	%	%	%	%	%
A sense of personal worth, self-respect	80	17	1	1	*	1
Recognition by one's peers	58	36	4	1	*	1
Being able to contribute to society	56	33	6	3	1	1
Approval by spouse	46	35	8	5	2	4
Approval by parents	22	41	14	11	7	5
Recognition by the public	14	46	19	16	4	1
Money to buy or do anything	8	34	25	24	8	1
Personal power	4	33	19	29	13	2
Social status	4	36	20	28	10	2
Expensive belongings, car, home, etc.	3	22	18	36	19	2

PERCEIVED REWARDS OF SUCCESS (continued)

EXTENT TO WHICH REWARDS ACHIEVED

To what extent do you feel that you, yourself, have achieved the various rewards of success listed below. To indicate this would you circle a number for each reward, the higher the number the closer you feel you are to attaining the reward, the lower the number, the farther from attaining the reward.

	TOTAL	OCCUPATION			INCOME				PERCEIVED DEGREE OF SUCCESS			
		Educa-tion	Other Pro-fess'n	Busi-ness	$200K & over	$100K-199K	$50K-99K	Under $50K	High-est (10)	Very High (9)	High (8)	Not so High (7 & Under)
	%	%	%	%	%	%	%	%	%	%	%	%
Approval by spouse												
Mostly achieved (9,10)	59	58	63	59	66	60	59	52	73	70	53	40
Partly achieved (6-8)	28	28	24	33	24	28	30	26	17	20	36	32
Sense of personal worth												
Mostly achieved (9,10)	59	58	63	61	66	59	58	59	85	78	48	31
Partly achieved (6-8)	36	38	34	34	31	35	40	34	12	20	50	54
Approval by parents												
Mostly achieved (9,10)	53	53	55	57	61	54	52	50	60	65	47	38
Partly achieved (6-8)	24	24	25	24	19	23	27	19	16	17	29	29
Recognition by peers												
Mostly achieved (9,10)	45	44	51	45	47	49	45	40	72	69	30	17
Partly achieved (6-8)	49	51	45	50	48	48	51	49	24	30	67	65
Contributing to society												
Mostly achieved (9,10)	33	35	36	27	26	36	35	32	54	44	24	15
Partly achieved (6-8)	48	51	48	49	46	49	48	51	30	42	58	53
Recognition by public												
Mostly achieved (9,10)	17	13	16	16	19	18	15	21	34	24	10	7
Partly achieved (6-8)	41	39	41	54	40	47	40	38	31	44	43	42
Money do anything												
Mostly achieved (9,10)	11	5	12	18	28	17	3	4	28	13	5	6
Partly achieved (6-8)	39	35	42	50	52	45	38	21	36	41	44	24
Social status												
Mostly achieved (9,10)	10	10	9	13	15	14	8	6	24	11	7	6
Partly achieved (6-8)	51	50	54	57	57	52	52	45	46	57	52	42
Expensive belongings												
Mostly achieved (9,10)	9	4	10	14	21	13	3	3	19	11	5	4
Partly achieved (6-8)	39	32	43	50	49	48	38	16	38	42	41	25
Personal power												
Mostly achieved (9,10)	6	4	7	6	11	9	4	*	14	10	2	1
Partly achieved (6-8)	41	34	42	53	50	51	37	30	47	43	42	26

PERCEIVED REWARDS OF SUCCESS (continued)

		OCCUPATION				INCOME			PERCEIVED DEGREE OF SUCCESS			
	TOTAL	Educa-tion	Other profes-sional	Busi-ness	$200K & over	$100K-199K	$50K 99K	Under $50K	High-est (10)	Very High (9)	High (8)	Not so high (7 & Under)
	%	%	%	%	%	%	%	%	%	%	%	%
A sense of personal worth, self-respect												
Important (6-10)	97	99	98	96	98	97	98	96	96	99	98	91
Very important (9,10)	80	83	81	79	85	77	82	79	86	89	77	72
Recognition by one's peers												
Important (6-10)	94	95	95	92	90	94	96	90	92	97	96	88
Very important (9,10)	58	65	57	52	56	56	64	49	69	72	52	41
Being able to contribute to society												
Important (6-10)	89	92	91	85	93	90	91	91	90	93	90	92
Very important (9,10)	56	61	58	45	47	56	57	63	71	63	49	47
Approval by spouse												
Important (6-10)	81	81	82	89	87	83	83	82	80	85	82	75
Very important (9,10)	46	41	49	52	55	50	44	41	59	53	41	37
Approval by parents												
Important (6-10)	64	61	46	75	78	64	63	66	63	67	64	59
Very Important (9,10)	22	18	23	29	30	23	19	25	31	25	20	19
Recognition by the public												
Important (6-10)	60	55	62	60	57	59	59	55	61	65	59	50
Very Important (9,10)	14	12	12	13	8	15	15	16	23	17	10	13
Money to buy or do anything												
Important (6-10)	42	30	44	62	64	54	34	24	43	45	41	31
Very Important (9,10)	8	2	10	15	17	11	4	2	12	8	6	10
Personal power												
Important (6-10)	38	27	44	51	51	46	33	25	28	43	39	35
Very Important (9,10)	4	2	5	7	10	5	3	1	6	5	4	4
Social status												
Important (6-10)	40	36	41	47	44	46	40	40	36	46	41	36
Very Important (9,10)	4	3	6	4	5	5	4	2	7	4	4	4
Expensive belongings, car, home, etc.												
Important (6-10)	25	14	28	39	42	35	17	13	24	27	24	26
Very Important (9,10)	3	1	5	3	5	5	2	*	4	2	3	4

PERCEIVED REWARDS OF SUCCESS (continued)

	MOSTLY ACHIEVED (9,10)	PARTLY ACHIEVED (6-8)	UNACHIEVED (0-5)	TOTAL
	%	%	%	%
A sense of personal worth	60	37	3	100
Recognition by peers	47	49	4	100
Contribution to society	37	51	12	100
Approval by spouse	66	29	5	100
Approval by parents	67	23	10	100
Recognition by public	26	53	21	100
Money to buy or do anything	16	57	27	100
Personal power	11	67	22	100
Social status	15	69	16	100
Expensive belongings	18	61	21	100

PERSONAL HAPPINESS

How happy would you say you are, very happy, fairly happy or not too happy?

		RATED VERY IMPORTANT (9-10)										
		OCCUPATION			INCOME				PERCEIVED DEGREE OF SUCCESS			
	TOTAL	Educa-tion	Other profes-sional	Busi-ness	$200K & over	$100K-199K	$50K-99K	Under $50K	High-est (10)	Very High (9)	High (8)	Not so High (7 & Under)
	%	%	%	%	%	%	%	%	%	%	%	%
Very happy	53	52	56	61	61	57	52	44	71	64	46	36
Fairly happy	41	43	39	36	35	39	43	46	25	31	49	56
Not too happy	2	2	3	1	1	2	2	4	1	1	3	4
Undesignated	4	3	2	2	3	2	3	6	3	4	2	4
	100	100	100	100	100	100	100	100	100	100	100	100

FACTORS CONTRIBUTING TO SUCCESS

Listed below under general headings are FACTORS that are often mentioned as CONTRIBUTING to success in one's chosen field. Would you indicate how important you feel each factor has been in your own case by rating it on a scale from zero to ten—the more important the higher the number, the lower the number the less important you feel it is?

PRE-CAREER

PERSONAL CHARACTERISTICS OR TRAITS

	Rated Very Important (9-10) %
Being a hard worker	70
Common Sense	61
Not being afraid to pursue new ideas, ventures, take risks	56
Caring about other people	51
Not being afraid to be different	44
Intelligence	43
Ambition, desire to get ahead	43
Tolerance of other viewpoints	36
Having a broad range of interests	35
Special talent in specific area	33
Establishing well-defined personal goals	32

ACADEMIC EXPERIENCE

Desire to excel	58
Good work habits, ability to organize time, get things done	53
Having natural learning ability	46
Working hard at school work	42
Getting good grades	32
Attending high-quality school(s)	31
Influence and encouragement of teachers	31
Having specific academic goals	26
Scoring well on achievement tests	25
Involvement in extracurricular activities	16
Involvement in sports	5

FAMILY ENVIRONMENT & INFLUENCE

Happiness of home life	33
Strong support of parents	31
Strong support of family members	28
Physical environment or habitat when young	23
A strong religious upbringing	16
National ancestry, parents' ancestors, nationality	12
Important personal contacts	10
Material advantages, money, property	3

OUTSIDE SCHOOL ACTIVITIES

	Rated Very Important (9-10) %
Having a broad range of interests	22
Having outside jobs, summer work	20

COMPOSITE

Being a hard worker	70
Common Sense	61
Desire to excel (at school)	58
Good work habits	53
Caring about people	51
Natural learning ability	46
Not afraid to be different	44
Intelligence	43
Ambition, desire to get ahead	43
Working hard at school work	42

IN PRESENT CAREER

EXPERIENCE IN CHOSEN FIELD

Ability to get things done	68
Hard work, diligence	67
Ambition, desire to get ahead	51
Ability to motivate subordinates	41
Luck, timing, being at the right place at the right time	38
Respect for peers	37
Organizational ability	35
Special talent in chosen field	33
Choosing right field at right time	31
Having long-time interest in the field	26
Ability to follow instructions	22
A boss, superiors who assisted or advised	20
Supportive co-workers	17
Desire to make money	8

FACTORS CONTRIBUTING TO SUCCESS (continued)
PERSONAL CHARACTERISTICS OR TRAITS

Listed below under general headings are FACTORS that are often mentioned as CONTRIBUT-ING to success in one's chosen field. Would you indicate how important you feel each factor has been *in your own case* by rating it on a scale from zero to ten—the more important the higher the number, the lower the number the less important you feel it is.

	IMPORTANCE RATING					
	Very Important (9-10)	Fairly Important (6-8)	Neither Important nor Unimportant (5)	Fairly Unimportant (2-4)	Very Unimportant (0-1)	No Opinion
	%	%	%	%	%	%
Being a hard worker	70	24	2	1	1	2
Common Sense	61	33	3	1	1	1
Not being afraid to pursue new ideas, ventures, take risks	56	33	5	4	1	1
Caring about other people	51	34	6	5	2	2
Not being afraid to be different	44	40	8	6	1	1
Intelligence	43	52	3	1	*	1
Ambition, desire to get ahead	43	39	9	6	2	1
Tolerance of other viewpoints	36	47	9	6	1	1
Having a broad range of interests	35	46	10	7	1	1
Special talent in specific area	33	47	12	6	1	1
Establishing well-defined personal goals	32	42	12	10	3	1

RATED VERY IMPORTANT (9-10)

		OCCUPATION			INCOME				PERCEIVED DEGREE OF SUCCESS			
	TOTAL	Educa-tion	Other Pro-fess'n	Busi-ness	$200K & over	$100K-199K	$50K-99K	Under $50K	High-est (10)	Very High (9)	High (8)	Not so High (7 & Under)
	%	%	%	%	%	%	%	%	%	%	%	%
Being a hard worker	70	72	67	70	72	72	72	64	75	82	66	53
Common sense	61	55	68	71	70	62	60	57	77	72	55	47
Not being afraid to pursue new ideas, ventures, take risks	56	58	55	53	58	54	58	57	78	65	50	38
Caring about other people	51	46	54	57	54	55	47	54	67	60	47	27
Not being afraid to be different	44	45	44	41	40	41	46	52	68	54	34	33
Intelligence	43	51	43	32	39	36	47	43	56	54	37	26
Ambition, desire to get ahead	43	39	45	47	56	49	39	37	46	54	38	36
Tolerance of other viewpoints	36	38	37	37	35	31	37	45	46	44	33	19
Having a broad range of interests	35	35	36	30	29	34	35	40	45	43	28	24
Special talent in specific area	33	39	31	17	26	28	35	42	44	41	27	25
Establishing well-defined personal goals	32	33	30	30	30	33	31	40	42	39	29	22

FACTORS CONTRIBUTING TO SUCCESS (continued)
FAMILY ENVIRONMENT & INFLUENCE

Listed below under general headings are FACTORS that are often mentioned as CONTRIBUT-ING to success in one's chosen field. Would you indicate how important you feel each factor has been *in your own case* by rating it on a scale from zero to ten—the more important the higher the number, the lower the number the less important you feel it is.

IMPORTANCE RATING

	Very Important (9-10)	Fairly Important (6-8)	Neither Important nor Unimportant (5)	Fairly Unimportant (2-4)	Very Unimportant (0-1)	No Opinion
	%	%	%	%	%	%
Happiness of home life	33	41	11	11	3	1
Strong support of parents	31	38	11	14	4	2
Strong support of family members	28	35	12	16	7	2
Physical environment or habitat when young	23	43	14	15	4	1
A strong religious upbringing	16	24	11	24	24	1
Important personal contacts	12	33	15	25	14	1
National ancestry, parents' ancestors, nationality	10	25	18	27	18	2
Material advantages, money, property	3	18	16	43	19	1

RATED VERY IMPORTANT (9-10)

		OCCUPATION				INCOME			PERCEIVED DEGREE OF SUCCESS			
	TOTAL	Educa-tion	Other Pro-fess'n	Busi-ness	$200K & over	$100K-199K	$50K-99K	Under $50K	High-est (10)	Very High (9)	High (8)	Not so High (7 & Under)
	%	%	%	%	%	%	%	%	%	%	%	%
Happiness of home life	33	33	37	32	36	36	32	36	44	42	28	24
Strong support of parents	31	33	34	29	29	33	31	38	35	37	28	28
Strong support of family members	28	28	28	25	26	29	25	37	31	35	23	22
Physical environment or habitat when young	23	25	23	20	19	24	23	29	22	28	21	22
A strong religious upbringing	16	13	20	19	16	16	14	21	18	17	15	15
Important personal contacts	12	12	10	12	9	9	12	16	13	14	9	13
National ancestry, parents' ancestors, nationality	10	12	9	7	6	11	10	16	12	11	9	12
Material advantages, money, property	3	2	3	3	3	3	3	1	3	3	1	6

FACTORS CONTRIBUTING TO SUCCESS (continued)
ACADEMIC EXPERIENCE

Listed below under general headings are FACTORS that are often mentioned as CONTRIBUT-
ING to success in one's chosen field. Would you indicate how important you feel each factor
has been *in your own case* by rating it on a scale from zero to ten—the more important the
higher the number, the lower the number the less important you feel it is.

IMPORTANCE RATING

	Very Important (9-10)	Fairly Important (6-8)	Neither Important nor Unimportant (5)	Fairly Unimportant (2-4)	Very Unimportant (0-1)	No Opinion
	%	%	%	%	%	%
Desire to excel	58	31	4	3	1	3
Good work habits, ability to organize time, get things done	53	35	4	4	1	3
Having natural learning ability	46	44	5	2	*	3
Working hard at school work	42	41	7	5	2	3
Getting good grades	32	51	8	4	2	3
Influence and encouragement of teachers	31	48	8	8	2	3
Attending high-quality school(s)	31	41	11	10	5	2
Having specific academic goals	26	41	13	12	4	4
Scoring well on achievement tests	25	45	11	9	5	5
Involvement in extracurricular activities	16	35	15	18	12	4
Involvement in sports	5	22	13	26	31	3

RATED VERY IMPORTANT (9-10)

	OCCUPATION				INCOME				PERCEIVED DEGREE OF SUCCESS			
	TOTAL	Educa-tion	Other profes-sional	Busi-ness	$200K & over	$100K-199K	$50K-99K	Under $50K	High-est (10)	Very High (9)	High (8)	Not so High (7 & Under)
	%	%	%	%	%	%	%	%	%	%	%	%
Desire to excel	58	57	60	59	63	62	58	49	65	68	52	45
Good work habits, ability to organize time, get things done	53	59	55	49	54	54	56	48	61	63	51	37
Having natural learning ability	46	54	41	38	42	43	51	43	50	51	45	33
Working hard at school work	42	56	39	30	32	41	47	45	45	52	41	24
Getting good grades	32	45	31	18	23	32	37	29	37	38	30	21
Attending high-quality school(s)	31	34	33	25	29	33	31	30	44	33	27	24
Influence and encouragement of teachers	31	39	28	22	19	26	35	41	37	38	26	23
Having specific academic goals	26	37	25	15	17	30	28	29	30	34	24	18
Scoring well on achievement tests	25	33	25	16	21	26	28	20	27	32	21	17
Involvement in extracuricular activities	16	12	16	19	20	18	14	15	21	22	11	8
Involvement in sports	5	4	7	7	9	6	4	4	8	8	4	2

FACTORS CONTRIBUTING TO SUCCESS (continued)
OUTSIDE SCHOOL INTERESTS

Listed below under general headings are FACTORS that are often mentioned as CONTRIBUT-ING to success in one's chosen field. Would you indicate how important you feel each factor has been *in your own case* by rating it on a scale from zero to ten—the more important the higher the number, the lower the number the less important you feel it is.

IMPORTANCE RATING

	Very Important (9-10)	Fairly Important (6-8)	Neither Important nor Unimportant (5)	Fairly Unimportant (2-4)	Very Unimportant (0-1)	No Opinion
	%	%	%	%	%	%
Having a broad range of interests	22	47	13	11	5	2
Having outside jobs, summer work, etc.	20	42	11	15	9	3

RATED VERY IMPORTANT (9-10)

	OCCUPATION				INCOME				PERCEIVED DEGREE OF SUCCESS			
	TOTAL	Education	Other profes-sional	Busi-ness	$200K & over	$100K-199K	$50K-99K	Under $50K	High-est (10)	Very High (9)	High (8)	Not so High (7 & Under)
	%	%	%	%	%	%	%	%	%	%	%	%
Having a broad range of interests	22	18	27	24	26	21	20	28	25	30	17	17
Having outside jobs, summer work, etc.	20	18	21	26	20	21	21	21	21	26	17	17

219

FACTORS CONTRIBUTING TO SUCCESS (continued)
EXPERIENCE IN CHOSEN FIELD

Listed below under general headings are FACTORS that are often mentioned as CONTRIBUT-
ING to success in one's chosen field. Would you indicate how important you feel each factor
has been *in your own case* by rating it on a scale from zero to ten—the more important the
higher the number, the lower the number the less important you feel it is.

IMPORTANCE RATING

	Very Important (9-10)	Fairly Important (6-8)	Neither Important nor Unimportant (5)	Fairly Unimportant (2-4)	Very Unimportant (0-1)	No Opinion
	%	%	%	%	%	%
Ability to get things done	68	26	2	1	1	2
Hard work, diligence	67	26	2	1	1	3
Ambition, desire to get ahead	51	38	4	3	1	3
Ability to motivate subordinates	41	39	6	6	5	3
Luck, timing, being at the right place at the right time	38	43	7	7	2	3
Respect for peers	37	48	7	5	1	2
Organizational ability	35	44	8	7	3	3
Special talent in chosen field	33	51	9	5	*	2
Choosing right field at the right time	31	41	12	9	4	3
Having long-time interest in the field	26	39	13	14	5	3
Ability to follow instructions	22	46	12	12	5	3
A boss, superiors who assisted or advised	20	48	10	14	5	3
Supportive co-workers	17	52	12	12	4	3
Desire to make money	8	29	16	29	15	3

FACTORS CONTRIBUTING TO SUCCESS (continued)

RATED VERY IMPORTANT (9-10)

	TOTAL	OCCUPATION			INCOME				PERCEIVED DEGREE OF SUCCESS			
		Educa-tion	Other profes-sional	Busi-ness	$200K & over	$100K-199K	$50K-99K	Under $50K	High-est (10)	Very High (9)	High (8)	Not so High (7 & Under)
	%	%	%	%	%	%	%	%	%	%	%	%
Ability to get things done	68	66	71	73	74	72	70	57	83	80	63	49
Hard work, diligence	67	68	70	66	76	65	69	62	73	81	61	51
Ambition, desire to get ahead	51	46	52	61	64	54	51	42	63	63	44	37
Ability to motivate subordinates	41	33	45	58	57	47	37	32	58	51	36	24
Luck, timing, being at the right place at the right time	38	37	35	42	45	39	37	31	44	41	33	37
Respect for peers	37	34	39	39	37	39	35	42	49	44	33	24
Organizational ability	35	33	35	44	40	39	34	29	49	45	28	19
Special talent in chosen field	33	41	31	18	24	29	38	38	44	40	27	26
Choosing right field at right time	31	34	28	27	29	29	34	28	37	36	27	26
Having long-time interest in field	26	31	23	15	16	24	27	37	32	30	21	22
Ability to follow instructions	22	17	27	24	26	23	19	29	31	29	17	14
A boss, superiors who assisted or advised	20	20	20	20	20	21	20	20	29	23	19	13
Supportive co-workers	17	17	19	19	18	17	17	19	28	21	13	10
Desire to make money	8	1	9	20	23	13	3	2	8	10	6	8

FAMILY ENVIRONMENT AND INFLUENCES

DEGREE OF HAPPINESS AS CHILD

How happy a childhood did you have—very happy, fairly happy, fairly unhappy, very unhappy?

Very happy	33%
Fairly happy	53
Fairly unhappy	12
Very unhappy	1
Undesignated	1
	100%

SIBLINGS

Number of children in family
How many children were there in your family when you were growing up?

One	16%
Two	33
Three	24
Four	10
Five	7
Six or more	4
Undesignated	6
	100%

First born, last born
(UNLESS ONLY CHILD) Were you the oldest or youngest in your family?

Yes, oldest	34%
Yes, youngest	27
Neither	20
Only child	16
Undesignated	3
	100%

PARENTAL RELATIONSHIP

How well did you get along with your father—very well, fairly well, not too well, not at all?—your mother?

	FATHER	MOTHER
Very well	46%	64%
Fairly well	37	28
Not too well	10	5
Not at all well	2	1
Undesignated	5	2
	100%	100%

PARENTAL BACKGROUND

Education
How far in school did your father go?...your mother?

	FATHER	MOTHER
Graduate school	21%	5%
College	22	27
High school	27	41
Grade school	27	23
Undesignated	3	4
	100%	100%

FAMILY FINANCIAL SITUATION

How would you categorize your family's financial situation when you were growing up?

Very wealthy	2%
Wealthy	5
Above average	26
Average	30
Below average	20
Poor	12
Very poor	3
Undesignated	2
	100%

PERSONAL GOALS

LIFE GOALS

Have you always had pretty clear goals for your life, or not?

Yes	64%
No	33
Undesignated	3
	100%

PERSONS INFLUENCING LIFE GOALS

Parents
To what extent did your parents influence your life goals—a great deal, somewhat, hardly at all, or not at all?

A great deal	28%
Somewhat	41
Hardly at all	20
Not at all	8
Undesignated	3
	100%

Other People
When you were growing up, were there any other persons (other than your parents) who had a great deal of influence on you and your goals in life?

Yes	63%
No	37
	100%

CAREER GOALS

Have you always had pretty clear goals for your *career,* or not?

Yes	64%
No	33
Undesignated	3
	100%

THE SCHOOL YEARS

Measures of Performance
Class Standing
What was your standing in your senior year in high school? That is, in what percentile were you? For example, the top tenth, bottom quarter, etc.?

What was your class standing in your senior year of college?

THE SCHOOL YEARS

Class Standing

		OCCUPATION			INCOME				PERCEIVED DEGREE OF SUCCESS			
	TOTAL	Educa-tion	Other Profes-sional	Busi-ness	$200K & over	$100K-199K	$50K-99K	Under $50K	High-est (10)	Very High (9)	High (8)	Not so High (7 & Under)
	%	%	%	%	%	%	%	%	%	%	%	%
IN HIGH SCHOOL												
Top Tenth	66	74	66	65	58	65	71	62	63	68	69	56
#1	10	13	8	8	12	7	11	8	11	11	9	8
#2-5	13	14	14	13	13	12	14	12	14	12	12	15
Over #5	43	47	44	44	33	46	46	42	38	45	48	33
IN COLLEGE												
Top Tenth	49	61	47	44	48	51	51	42	45	51	52	42
#1	6	8	6	2	6	5	7	4	4	8	5	5
#2-5	13	18	12	12	17	11	14	10	13	15	13	12
Over #5	30	35	29	30	25	35	30	28	28	28	34	25

	IN HIGH SCHOOL Top Tenth					IN COLLEGE Top Tenth			
	TOTAL	#1	#2-5	Over #5		TOTAL	#1	#2-5	Over #5
	%	%	%	%		%	%	%	%
TOTAL	66	10	13	43	TOTAL	49	6	13	30
OCCUPATION					**OCCUPATION**				
Education	74	13	14	47	Education	61	8	18	35
Other Professional	66	8	14	44	Other Professional	47	6	12	29
Business	65	8	13	44	Business	44	2	12	30
INCOME					**INCOME**				
$200K & Over	58	12	13	33	$200K & Over	48	6	17	25
$100K-199K	65	7	12	46	$100K-199K	51	5	11	35
$50K-99K	71	11	14	46	$50K-99K	51	7	14	30
Under $50K	62	8	12	42	Under $50K	42	4	10	28

ACADEMICS

Measures of Performance
IQ Tests
Have you ever taken an IQ test?

Yes	76%
No	22
Undesignated	2
	100%

(IF YES) Do you recall what your score was?

Under 100	*
110-119	2%
120-129	5
130-139	13
140-149	10
150-159	4
160-169	3
170-179	1
180 & Over	2
Unspecified	60
	100%

GRADES

How important was it to your parents that you get good grades—very important, fairly important, not very important, or not at all important?

Very important	35%
Fairly important	50
Not very important	11
Not at all important	2
Undesignated	2
	100%

Were you rewarded in any way by your parents for getting *good* grades…Punished for getting *bad* grades?

	Rewarded for good grades	Punished for bad grades
Yes	23%	7%
No	75	90
Undesignated	2	3
	100%	100%

Were your grades about the same for all of your courses or were they higher in some courses than in others?

All about the same	33%
Better in some courses	63
Undesignated	4
	100%

Grades

		OCCUPATION				INCOME				PERCEIVED DEGREE OF SUCCESS			
	TOTAL	Educa-tion	Other Profes-sional	Busi-ness	$200K & over	$100K-199K	$50K-99K	Under $50K	High-est (10)	Very High (9)	High (8)	Not so High (7 & under)
	%	%	%	%	%	%	%	%	%	%	%	%
All about same	33	42	37	25	28	37	33	32	36	37	34	23
Higher in some	63	56	61	71	70	60	65	61	61	60	62	76
Undesignated	4	2	2	4	2	3	2	7	3	3	4	1
	100	100	100	100	100	100	100	100	100	100	100	100

FAVORITE TEACHERS

Did you ever have a teacher or teachers who made you enthusiastic about a particular subject?

Yes	89%
No	9
Undesignated	2
	100%

SCHOLARSHIPS

Did you have a scholarship(s) when you were in college?…In graduate school?

	In College	In Graduate School
Yes	44%	46%
No	48	35
Did not attend	5	19
Undesignated	3	*
	100%	100%

	TOTAL	OCCUPATION Educa-tion	OCCUPATION Other Profes-sional	OCCUPATION Busi-ness	INCOME $200K & over	INCOME $100K-199K	INCOME $50K-99K	INCOME Under $50K	PERCEIVED DEGREE OF SUCCESS High-est (10)	PERCEIVED DEGREE OF SUCCESS Very High (9)	PERCEIVED DEGREE OF SUCCESS High (8)	PERCEIVED DEGREE OF SUCCESS Not so High (7 & under)
	%	%	%	%	%	%	%	%	%	%	%	%
In College	44	58	39	30	30	43	49	44	44	46	46	36
In Graduate school	46	71	43	25	21	38	61	47	46	47	49	40

EXTRA-CURRICULAR ACTIVITIES

Athletics
Were you on any athletic teams in high school? In college?

	In High School	In College
Yes	50%	29%
No	49	68
Undesignated	1	3
	100%	100%

Non-Athletic
Other than sports, what extra-curricular activities, if any, were you involved in high school? In college?

	In High School	In College
Yes, involved	80%	71%
No, not involved	20	29
	100%	100%

Leadership Role
Were you an officer of your class, any school (college) organization, or a team captain of any athletic team in high school? In college?

	In High School	In College
Yes	58%	46%
No	40	50
Undesignated	2	4
	100%	100%

NON-ACADEMIC INTERESTS

Special Interests
Outside of school and any job you might have had while in high school, what special interests, if any, did you have? How about when you were in college?

	In High School	In College
Had special interests	73%	70%
Did not have special interests	27	30
	100%	100%

READING HABITS

Outside of school how much reading did you do in *your early years,* that is, *before the age of 10*— much more than other kids the same age, somewhat more, about the same amount, somewhat less, or much less?

Outside of your school, how much reading did you do during *your high school years*—much more than other students the same age, somewhat more, about the same amount, somewhat less, or much less?

Outside of your required school reading, how much reading did you do during *your college* years—much more than other students the same age, somewhat more, about the same amount, somewhat less, or much less?

	Before age of 10	In High School	In College
More	73%	73%	59%
Much more	47%	42%	25%
Somewhat more	26	31	34
Less	7	7	9
Much less	6	6	8
Somewhat less	1	1	1
About Same Amount	19	19	28
Undesignated	1	1	4
	100	100	100

Impact of book(s) on life
What books would you say have had the greatest impact on your life?

Named a book(s)	63%
Did not name book(s)	37
	100%

225

THE SCHOOL YEARS (continued)

		OCCUPATION				INCOME			PERCEIVED DEGREE OF SUCCESS			
	TOTAL	Educa-tion	Other Profes-sional	Busi-ness	$200K & over	$100K-199K	$50K-99K	Under $50K	High-est (10)	Very High (9)	High (8)	Not so High (7 & under)
	%	%	%	%	%	%	%	%	%	%	%	%
Read Much More:												
In early years	47	53	49	35	44	44	50	42	46	47	45	45
In High School	42	47	45	26	36	38	46	40	43	44	37	43
In College	25	30	23	16	20	24	30	22	28	29	23	22

JOB EXPERIENCE

Did you have any part-time or full-time jobs when you were in high school? In college?

	In High School	In College
Yes	70%	77%
No	28	19
Undesignated	2	4
	100%	100%

NUMBER OF FRIENDS

Would you say you had an average number of friends when you were of high school age/in college, more than average, or were you somewhat of a loner?

	In High School	In College
More than average	24%	24%
Fewer than average	21	17
Average	49	52
Somewhat of a loner	5	3
Undesignated	1	4
	100%	100%

		OCCUPATION				INCOME			PERCEIVED DEGREE OF SUCCESS			
	TOTAL	Educa-tion	Other Profes-sional	Busi-ness	$200K & over	$100K 199K	$50K-99K	Under $50K	High-est (10)	Very High (9)	High (8)	Not so High (7 & Under)
	%	%	%	%	%	%	%	%	%	%	%	%
In High School												
More than average	24	20	26	30	32	29	22	18	26	27	26	13
Fewer than average	21	25	17	19	16	20	24	20	23	20	20	25
In College												
More than average	24	21	28	26	33	27	22	19	29	26	24	16
Fewer than average	17	20	19	15	15	17	18	17	18	14	16	27

PERSONAL CAREER

EXISTENCE OF CAREER GOALS

Have you always had pretty clear goals for your career or not?

Yes	64%
No	33
Undesignated	3
	100%

NUMBER OF FIELDS EMPLOYED IN

Have you held jobs in fields other than your present field?

Yes	57%
No	40
Undesignated	3
	100%

APTITUDE FOR FIELD

As Successful in Another Field
Do you feel you would have been successful in another field or not?

Yes	81%
No	5
Undesignated	14
	100%

Aptitude Test/Aptitude for Current Field
Did you ever take a test to determine what you had an aptitude or aptitudes for? (IF YES) Did it show you had an aptitude in your present field or not?

Yes	48%
Have aptitude	33
Don't have	7
Can't recall	8
No	49
Can't recall	3
	100%

ENTER SAME FIELD AGAIN?

If you had your career to enter over again, would you do so?

Yes	83%
No	8
Undesignated	9
	100%

PERCEIVED TALENTS AND ATTRIBUTES

Looking at myself as objectively as I can (or as some other person would), I would give myself the following grade for each of the following areas:

	A			B				C	D	FAIL	
	TOTAL	A+	A	A−	TOTAL	B+	B	B−	TOTAL	TOTAL	TOTAL	UNDESIGNATED
	%	%	%	%	%	%	%	%	%	%	%
Common sense	79	20	40	19	17	11	5	1	1	-	*	3
Self-reliance	77	21	40	16	18	9	7	2	2	*	*	3
General intelligence	75	12	42	21	22	14	7	1	1	*	*	2
Specialized knowledge required in field	74	20	36	18	22	13	8	1	2	*	*	2
Ability to get things done	74	20	36	18	21	10	8	3	2	*	*	3
Getting along with others	68	16	34	18	28	17	9	2	2	*	*	2
Leadership ability	67	14	30	23	26	15	9	2	5	*	*	2
Writing skill	67	21	29	17	27	15	9	3	4	*	*	2
Ability to put orders from superiors into effect	65	10	33	22	24	14	9	1	4	*	*	7
Reading skill	64	20	28	16	28	14	10	4	5	*	*	3
Public speaking ability	64	17	30	17	28	14	11	3	5	1	*	2
Creativity, inventiveness	63	16	28	19	29	14	11	4	4	*	*	4
Intuition	63	16	28	19	29	15	11	3	4	*	*	4
Willpower	63	18	28	17	29	14	10	5	5	*	*	3
Organizational ability	62	14	30	18	30	15	12	3	6	*	*	2
Self-confidence	61	12	30	19	33	16	14	3	4	*	*	2
Work habits	59	13	26	20	32	15	13	4	6	1	*	2
Conversational ability	57	14	28	15	33	16	12	5	7	*	*	3
Ability to motivate subordinates	56	9	26	21	35	18	13	4	5	*	*	4
Ability to make money	32	4	15	13	49	21	22	6	15	1	*	3

PERCEIVED TALENTS AND ATTRIBUTES (continued)
GRADED A

		OCCUPATION				INCOME			PERCEIVED DEGREE OF SUCCESS			
	TOTAL	Educa-tion	Other profes-sional	Busi-ness	$200K & over	$100K-199K	$50K-99K	Under $50K	High-est (10)	Very High (9)	High (8)	Not so High (7 & Under)
	%	%	%	%	%	%	%	%	%	%	%	%
Common sense	79	79	80	87	87	83	77	73	85	85	75	72
Self-reliance	77	81	79	82	85	79	78	68	88	84	75	63
General intelligence	75	78	76	75	74	76	77	70	81	81	74	60
Specialized knowledge required in field	74	80	74	65	64	73	77	81	85	80	72	58
Ability to get things done	74	74	78	80	80	80	76	60	87	83	71	58
Ability to get along with others	68	66	72	79	77	68	67	64	82	70	68	51
Leadership ability	67	62	74	77	82	73	63	57	82	79	62	46
Writing skill	67	70	68	63	65	69	66	70	74	67	68	59
Ability to put orders from superiors into effect	65	62	69	74	69	73	64	55	76	73	60	51
Reading skill	64	71	65	56	61	63	67	64	67	67	63	62
Public speaking ability	64	71	64	58	60	66	65	64	73	69	60	57
Creativity, inventiveness	63	64	63	58	63	62	64	65	75	67	59	57
Intuition	63	62	66	64	67	66	64	57	75	68	59	56
Willpower	63	64	68	65	70	69	61	56	79	69	58	53
Organizational ability	62	62	66	67	64	69	61	54	75	73	57	40
Self-confidence	61	61	62	68	72	67	59	49	78	75	55	35
Work habits	59	61	58	62	60	64	58	55	67	69	53	49
Conversational ability	57	57	59	57	58	58	57	55	73	59	53	49
Ability to motivate subordinates	56	50	58	73	74	63	52	40	69	70	50	32
Ability to make money	32	22	38	55	65	48	22	8	51	38	28	20

PERCEIVED PERSONAL CHARACTERISTICS

Would you indicate how accurately the following statements describe you personally—the higher the number you select the more you feel that statement describes you—the lower the number, the less accurately it describes you.

	AGREE		NEITHER AGREE NOR DISAGREE	DISAGREE		
	STRONGLY	NOT SO STRONGLY		STRONGLY	NOT SO STRONGLY	DON'T KNOW
	%	%	%	%	%	%
Strong sense of right and wrong	67	24	3	2	2	2
Belief in supreme being	43	16	8	11	19	3
Not afraid to be different	40	47	7	4	*	2
Care about others	38	46	8	5	1	2
Tolerance	36	52	6	4	*	2
Broad range of interests	35	46	9	7	1	2
Well defined goals	32	46	9	9	2	2
Not afraid to take risks	32	50	10	5	1	2
Belief that God has plan	22	13	9	14	38	4
Close personal relationship with God	21	16	9	14	36	4
Born lucky	10	27	20	24	15	4

RATED VERY IMPORTANT (9-10)

	OCCUPATION				INCOME				PERCEIVED DEGREE OF SUCCESS			
	TOTAL	Educa-tion	Other profes-sional	Busi-ness	$200K & over	$100K-199K	$50K-99K	Under $50K	High-est (10)	Very High (9)	High (8)	Not so High (7 & Under)
	%	%	%	%	%	%	%	%	%	%	%	%
Strong sense of right and wrong	67	64	75	72	73	69	64	71	78	73	63	59
Belief in supreme being	43	36	50	53	46	50	38	50	51	51	37	42
Not afraid to be different	40	42	42	32	39	40	39	49	62	46	32	28
Care about other people	38	41	39	38	32	39	39	47	54	45	34	24
Tolerance of other viewpoints	36	37	38	34	33	37	34	43	51	41	32	24
Broad range of interests	35	39	38	31	33	35	34	42	50	40	29	27
Well-defined personal goals	32	36	31	27	32	33	34	35	49	38	27	17
Not afraid to take chances or risks	32	28	34	30	39	28	32	32	51	41	23	18
Belief that God had a plan	22	17	27	29	21	27	19	30	30	28	19	20
Close personal relationship with God	21	18	26	25	22	24	17	27	27	27	17	19
Born lucky	10	9	11	10	14	11	7	11	20	10	7	8

SATISFACTION WITH INDIVIDUAL ASPECTS OF LIFE

Now, here are some questions concerning how satisfied or dissatisfied you are with various things about your life. To indicate this, would you circle the numbers below. If you are extremely satisfied with something, you would circle the highest number; If you are extremely dissatisfied, you would circle the lowest number, 0. If you are neither extremely satisfied nor extremely dissatisfied you would circle some number in between zero and ten.

	SATISFIED			DISSATISFIED			
	TOTAL (6-10)	VERY SATISFIED (9-10)	FAIRLY SATISFIED (6-8)	TOTAL (0-4)	VERY DISSATISFIED (0,1)	FAIRLY DISSATISFIED (2-4)	UNDESIGNATED (and 5)
	%	%	%	%	%	%	%
Your standard of living	92	53	39	3	1	2	5
Your education in preparing you for the work you do	90	60	30	3	1	2	7
The way things are going in your own personal life at this time	90	44	46	5	1	4	5
Your family life	87	51	36	6	1	5	7
Your job/the work you do	86	48	38	5	1	4	9
Your education in preparing you for life	86	49	37	5	1	4	9
The way you get along with your children	83	53	30	4	1	3	13
The way you get along with your spouse	82	58	24	5	2	3	13
Your free time/the time when you are not working at your job	82	39	43	8	1	7	10
The way things are going in this country at this time	52	5	47	33	5	28	15

SATISFACTION WITH INDIVIDUAL ASPECTS OF LIFE (continued)

	WHO'S WHO		U.S. PUBLIC	
	SATISFIED (6-10)	VERY SATISFIED (9,10)	SATISFIED (6-10)	VERY SATISFIED (9,10)
	%	%	%	%
Your standard of living	92	53	78	38
Your education in preparing you for the work you do	90	60	—	—
The way things are going in your own personal life at this time	90	44	79	40
Your family life	87	51	86	54
Your job/the work you do	86	48	70	38
Your education in preparing you for life	86	50	—	—
The way you get along with your children	83	53	—	—
The way you get along with your spouse	82	58	—	—
Your free time/the time when you are not working at your job	82	39	78	42
The way things are going in this country at this time	52	5	52	8

SATISFACTION WITH INDIVIDUAL ASPECTS OF LIFE (continued)

	TOTAL	OCCUPATION			INCOME				PERCEIVED DEGREE OF SATISFACTION			
		Educa-tion	Other profes-sional	Busi-ness	$200K & over	$100K-199K	$50K-99K	Under $50K	High-est (10)	Very High (9)	High (8)	Not so High (7 & Under)
	%	%	%	%	%	%	%	%	%	%	%	%
Your Standard of Living												
Satisfied (6-10)	92	93	94	95	96	96	95	82	96	96	93	81
Very satisfied (9,10)	53	52	55	62	74	60	48	39	68	67	47	28
Your Education In Preparing You For The Work You Do												
Satisfied (6-10)	90	94	96	85	87	94	92	85	93	93	90	84
Very satisfied (9,10)	60	69	64	55	58	64	63	50	72	71	55	42
The Way Things Are Going In Your Own Personal Life At This Time												
Satisfied (6-10)	90	91	92	91	93	95	91	81	94	92	91	84
Very satisfied (9,10)	44	47	45	45	49	44	45	36	59	55	38	19
Your Family Life												
Satisfied (6-10)	87	88	89	89	74	91	89	88	90	90	88	77
Very Satisfied (9,10)	51	53	55	55	56	52	52	44	68	60	47	29
Your Job/The Work You Do												
Satisfied (6-10)	86	88	90	85	87	92	89	74	90	90	87	78
Very satisfied (9,10)	48	51	50	47	52	51	48	42	73	61	38	28
Your Education In Preparing You For Life												
Satisfied (6-10)	86	91	90	83	88	89	88	79	86	91	88	76
Very satisfied (9,10)	50	55	51	47	52	52	51	40	61	61	44	31
The Way You Get Along With Your Children												
Satisfied (6-10)	83	84	88	90	86	86	85	74	90	88	83	69
Very satisfied (9,10)	53	55	55	55	54	53	54	52	65	60	50	38
The Way You Get Along With Your Spouse												
Satisfied (6-10)	82	85	82	88	87	85	85	68	82	90	83	71
Very satisfied (9,10)	58	61	60	62	61	57	60	52	67	65	55	44
Your Free Time/The Time When You Are Not Working At Your Job												
Satisfied (6-10)	82	83	84	83	88	80	85	78	86	83	84	72
Very satisfied (9,10)	39	42	42	33	36	39	41	38	53	43	37	22
The Way Things Are Going In This Country At This Time												
Satisfied (6-10)	52	42	60	72	73	61	47	34	54	56	51	46
Very satisfied (9,10)	5	4	5	6	6	8	3	2	9	6	3	3

PARTICIPATION IN CLUBS, ORGANIZATIONS, CHARITABLE ACTIVITIES

MEMBERSHIP IN ORGANIZATIONS

Do you happen to belong to any clubs or organizations?

Yes   81%
No   19
                                           ────
                                           100%

INVOLVEMENT IN CHARITABLE ACTIVITIES

Do you happen to be involved in any volunteer activities?

Yes   59%
No   41
                                           ────
                                           100%

	OCCUPATION				INCOME				PERCEIVED DEGREE OF SUCCESS			
	TOTAL	Educa-tion	Other profes-sional	Busi-ness	$200K & over	$100K-199K	$50K-99K	Under $50K	High-est (10)	Very High (9)	High (8)	Not so High (7 & Under)
	%	%	%	%	%	%	%	%	%	%	%	%
Any Voluntary Activities	59	52	64	69	69	62	54	63	60	61	58	52
Average # of hours	3.1	2.2	3.9	3.9	4.7	3.2	2.4	3.7	3.0	3.6	2.8	3.0
Donations: money, time Donated money	96	97	99	99	99	98	96	95	97	96	97	93
Given money to religious organization	68	64	79	78	70	73	68	65	74	72	67	63
Donated time to helping poor	43	38	48	52	49	47	40	42	46	45	41	39
Donated time to religious work	31	27	36	40	26	35	29	39	34	31	31	29
Written letter to political official or signed a political petition	72	75	70	79	76	72	71	74	73	73	74	66

233

INTERESTS AND ACTIVITIES

TV VIEWING

On a typical day how many hours do you spend watching television?

None	11%
1 hour-1 hr. 59 min.	43
2 hours-2 hrs. 59 min.	28
3 hours	8
Over 3 hours	4
Unspecified	6
	100%
Average	1.5 hours

BOOK READING

Do you happen to be reading a book at the present time?

Yes	75%
No	20
Undesignated	5
	100%

		OCCUPATION			INCOME				PERCEIVED DEGREE OF SUCCESS			
	TOTAL	Educa-tion	Other profes-sional	Busi-ness	$200K & over	$100K-199K	$50K-99K	Under $50K	High-est (10)	Very High (9)	High (8)	Not so High (7 & Under)
	%	%	%	%	%	%	%	%	%	%	%	%
Presently Reading Book	75	83	76	69	71	72	78	80	80	76	74	75
Read over 20 books in Last 12 months												
All books	26	36	19	14	17	21	31	30	23	26	26	31
Fiction	10	13	6	5	6	8	11	13	9	10	10	11
Non-Fiction	9	14	6	1	2	5	12	13	7	8	9	11
Average Number of books within last 12 months	#	#	#	#	#	#	#	#	#	#	#	#
All books	18	25	15	12	13	16	21	21	18	17	19	22
Fiction	9	11	7	7	7	8	9	10	8	8	9	9
Non-Fiction	10	14	8	5	6	8	12	11	10	9	10	13

MATERIAL REWARDS, COMFORTS, PLEASURES

<u>POSSESSIONS</u>
Which of these do you, or does your family own?

		OCCUPATION			INCOME				PERCEIVED DEGREE OF SUCCESS			
	TOTAL	Educa-tion	Other profes-sional	Busi-ness	$200K & over	$100K-199K	$50K-99K	Under $50K	High-est (10)	Very High (9)	High (8)	Not so High (7 & Under)
	%	%	%	%	%	%	%	%	%	%	%	%
Original paintings	66	67	65	63	70	67	65	64	67	65	68	64
Antiques	46	41	46	58	68	46	41	35	49	48	44	40
Exercise equipment	38	30	43	45	49	46	35	25	43	40	38	31
VCR	37	22	46	56	67	48	28	18	41	38	34	40
Two homes	35	26	34	48	61	41	26	23	38	36	33	31
Three or more cars	31	21	39	45	54	38	24	15	36	35	28	22
Swimming pool	15	7	21	22	41	16	7	8	18	17	13	13
Pool Table	13	9	17	17	25	15	10	7	12	11	14	13
Motor boat	12	9	15	18	19	13	11	7	13	14	10	11
Jacuzzi	9	4	9	17	23	10	5	4	12	10	7	8
Yacht	5	5	6	6	5	8	5	1	5	6	6	1
Tennis court	2	1	3	6	10	3	*	*	4	3	2	2
Paddle tennis court	1	1	1	2	3	1	1	*	1	2	1	1

WHO ARE THE SUCCESSFUL

Socio-Economic & Demographic
Characteristics

FIELD OF ENDEAVOR

What kind of business or industry are you
in and what kind of work to you do there?

Education, Teaching, Administration	31%
Business	18
Industry-Manufacturing	
Industry-Service	
Finance	
Law, Lawyers, Judges	13
Communications, the Media, Newspapers,	
Broadcasting Publishers	9
Science & Technology, Engineering	6
Military	5
Medicine, Health Care	3
Public Officials, Government	3
Visual Arts, Art, Architecture, Sculpture	2
Performing arts, Entertainers, Actors,	
Musicians, Theatre	1
Sports	*
Religion, Clergy	*
All Others	1
Undesignated	8
	100%

EDUCATION

What was the last grade you completed in school?

Ph.D	34%
Law Degree	10
M.D.	7
Masters, M.A.	9
Any graduate school	16
College graduate	11
Less than college graduate	4
High school graduate	4
Less than high school grad.	*
Undesignated	5
	100%

		OCCUPATION				INCOME			PERCEIVED DEGREE OF SUCCESS			
	TOTAL	Educa-tion	Other profes-sional	Busi-ness	$200K & over	$100K-199K	$50K-99K	Under $50K	High-est (10)	Very High (9)	High (8)	Not so High (7 & Under)
	%	%	%	%	%	%	%	%	%	%	%	%
Ph.D or equivalent	50	78	57	19	26	50	63	45	48	53	52	44
Graduate school	25	15	31	37	36	26	21	26	26	25	25	26
College graduate	11	1	4	24	21	10	8	9	9	11	10	14
Less than college graduate	9	3	4	16	12	9	5	14	12	7	8	11
Undesignated	5	3	4	4	5	5	3	6	5	4	5	5
	100	100	100	100	100	100	100	100	100	100	100	100

WHO ARE THE SUCCESSFUL (continued)

ANNUAL INCOME

	OCCUPATION				PERCEIVED DEGREE OF SUCCESS			
	TOTAL	Other Educa-tion	profes-sional	Busi-ness	High-est (10)	Very High (9)	High (8)	Not so High (7 & Under)
	%	%	%	%	%	%	%	%
$200,000 and over	16	2	18	42	1	*	2	7
$100,000-199,999	22	14	31	32	14	9	13	17
$50,000-99,999	45	66	41	20	33	48	47	44
$20,000-49,999	13	17	9	4	27	23	23	21
Under $20,000	2	*	*	1	21	19	13	10
Undesignated	2	1	1	1	4	1	2	1
	100	100	100	100	100	100	100	100

RELIGION

	OCCUPATION				INCOME				PERCEIVED DEGREE OF SUCCESS			
	TOTAL	Other Educa-tion	profes-sional	Busi-ness	$200K & over	$100K-199K	$50K-99K	Under $50K	High-est (10)	Very High (9)	High (8)	Not so High (7 & Under)
	%	%	%	%	%	%	%	%	%	%	%	%
Protestant	56	57	56	66	56	58	53	61	56	59	54	53
Catholic	12	7	14	16	14	16	10	11	11	15	11	12
Jewish	12	11	13	10	15	15	11	9	16	11	12	11
Other	7	9	2	3	3	6	10	6	7	5	9	5
None	4	5	9	1	4	1	5	4	4	1	5	6
Agnostic	1	1	1	1	1	1	1	2	*	2	1	1
Atheist	*	1	*	*	*	*	1	1	*	1	1	*
Undesignated	8	9	5	3	7	3	9	6	6	6	7	12
	100	100	100	100	100	100	100	100	100	100	100	100

INDEX